START HERE

—— THE ——
PROVEN BLUEPRINT
—— TO ——
LASTING BUSINESS
SUCCESS

TREMAIN DAVIS

Lightning Fast Book Publishing, LLC
P.O. Box 441328
Fort Washington, MD 20744

www.lfbookpublishing.com

LIGHTNING FAST
BOOK PUBLISHING

ISBN: 978-1-7348113-3-9

Table of Contents

Introduction

How do you build a skyscraper? The answer is simple, one brick at a time. As simple as this response is, it can be quite complex. Good ideas are easy to come by, but turning an idea into a successful business is hard. There are certain and specific steps that will take you from idea to execution, and making that connection from idea to successful business is very difficult without a blueprint. This book will give you the Vision to Value framework for business success. Each piece of Vision to Value builds off of the last until you have a solid foundation to build your empire. Simply put, these next 100 pages will change your business life. My easy to read and easy to understand system is guaranteed to take your business or idea to the next level!

I love talking about Vision to Value because I was once a young entrepreneur with a dream. The problem is that I did not know where to start. The things that I did and the advice I received from people were not always helpful. Nobody could tell me exactly what I needed to do "today" to move my ideas forward. This lack of understanding about the business basics caused me to be inefficient and largely ineffective with my early endeavors. It took failing, losing money, and wasting resources to learn the fundamental building blocks of business success. It took me 15 years to figure out how to properly build a business. Now that I've done it multiple times, I teach others how to do it. My Vision to Value framework will save you a lot of time and headache trying to figure out your next move.

The fundamental building blocks that underpin every business are the exact same. Vision to Value is a basic business framework that anyone in any type of business can immediately use at any point in their business life cycle. This framework is the starting point for all business. It takes you back to the basic fundamentals in a way that is easy to understand and implement. What I've discovered on this journey is that no-one teaches entrepreneurs and business leaders the basics of business. We literally have to go out and learn them on our own while trying to start a company. Then, after enough business blood has been spilled, we begin to get it. I am going to help you to avoid those missteps by teaching you the business basics. Even the most mature and successful businesses, as you will see, have to get back to basics to launch any new product, service or innovation. The best thing about this is you can use the principles in this book today. My framework will make it easy to assess your current business or start with an idea right now.

Finally, and most importantly, Vision to Value is a unified communications tool that allows people from any area of business to speak the same language. This makes developing business ideas a much more efficient process. There are many successful people in business who all have their own way of articulating their success narrative. While most of it is good, there aren't many tools out there that unify the core principles of these various avenues to business success. Vision to Value will give you, the reader, a common framework that is transferable to any area of business. This unified communications tool is a very effective tool that connects people and ideas, which is THE most potent combination for creativity on the planet. When you and your team can speak the same basic business language when discussing ideas, it drastically increases the chances for a successful outcome!

CHAPTER 1:

A Framework for Success

Why This Book Is Important

I am an entrepreneur and a student of business. I read and consume a mountain of information regarding this topic every year. I have learned from all the greats. But it's the experience of starting my own companies for the last 20 years that has given me the insights that make the difference. When I compare the information available on the subject of entrepreneurship and what I have experienced in real time there is a massive gap. One of the main things I've noticed is that it's not the information itself that's not available. It is the accessibility of the right information. It's there, it's just hard to find. Even if you do find some good information, there is no bell that rings or whistle that blows to tell you that this is good information for my business. The good stuff gets lost in a sea of business content, a lot of which is not very good. The funny thing, however, is that the bad stuff is often pushed by people who are great at social media and influencing; it gets all the clicks and views. For example, I've watched YouTube videos of some of the topics discussed in this book that were created years ago. Yet they only have a few thousand views. But of course, whatever is trending right now will have hundreds of millions of views. One of the key things that I've learned is where to find the stuff that matters and how to put it together in a meaningful way. So why aren't certain business concepts more mainstream? How do you find the information you need to be successful with your business? What is the path to get from here to there, from idea to market, from vision to value? These are the questions that we are definitely going to explore.

The average entrepreneur does not know what they don't know. Even worse, they don't know where to find out what they don't know. It really is a two-edged sword that can cut you on both sides. If you are a successful entrepreneur or a business owner of any size, you know exactly what I am talking about. There is so much trending information that it becomes very difficult to know what is good and what is junk. Your best teacher has probably been the trial and error of your own failures and successes. Because of technology and social media, the billionaires, major CEOs, and other highly successful people are more accessible than ever before. You can do a simple Google or YouTube search to hear any of them speak about their success and their journey. They give great nuggets of wisdom and great motivational content to push people forward. However, information about the foundational, structural things that every business needs to be successful is much more elusive.

The past 20 years have been the era of the entrepreneur. The ideologies that have framed the way we do business today are all relatively new. There are countless poetic stories of the small "David" startup defeating the "Goliath" in their industry. This has created the notion that anybody can start with an idea and become a massive success. This notion is great for the spirit of discovery and exploration for which this country was built on. The idea that anyone from any background can live their dream is amplified in today's business landscape.

The Vision to Value framework is based on time tested business strategy principles from people like Richard Remult, Mark Kramer, Michael Skok, Michael Porter, Steve Case, Eric Reis and Steve Blank. If you haven't heard of any of these people, don't worry, most people haven't. But these are the intellectuals who have literally led the transition into entrepreneurship over the last 20 years. They teach at schools like Harvard and Stanford and are responsible for investing in companies like Facebook, AOL, Youtube and Airbnb. These are the business titans who have worked in the background of major global business for many, many years. These are the people who have the entrepreneurial blueprint for what it takes to be successful on any business level.

But, as you can imagine, they are not trending on social media. Some are not even on social media. This is a huge problem because these people have the answers to all your questions as an entrepreneur. Because of this, many people will start business initiatives without having the right information. They will get a heavy dose of information that is trending on social media, Google, or maybe even their state's website. It's sad to say but most of this information will not help you develop your idea. I believe this is one major reason why over 75% of new businesses fail within the first 5 years. People just do not know where to find the business information that they need.

Vision to Value evens the playing field for everyone in business. The people I mentioned earlier, and many others, teach at the top universities or run hedge funds or assist with government economics. **But you should not have to get an MBA from Harvard to know how to start, build, maintain, grow, or innovate a business.** Taking a strategy approach to business and entrepreneurship is the most effective way to build a foundation for any kind of business idea or initiative. Whether you're a start-up or a well-established business, an entrepreneur or a careered employee, the Vision to Value framework will give you the tools you need to be successful. I'm bringing you the right information packaged up in an easy-to-manage format for your success. Million-dollar business ideas come by all the time, but I've learned that ideas truly are a dime a dozen. The real prize is when someone can turn an idea into a real business. This is where the Vision to Value framework will help you the most. The times we live in are becoming more and more conducive for people to take that leap into entrepreneurship.

There are tons of business "gurus" and motivational mindset content on how to believe in yourself to be successful. They say all you have to do is have the confidence to launch out there and things will be alright. They tell you to work hard and invest in yourself but none of this is helpful to actually develop the idea you have. Even state websites that give information about business formation and tax options are still not very helpful for someone who is looking for clear information on what they need to do right now. Anyone can pay the fee to the state to form a company. Picking an LLC or a Sole Propriety is not a very difficult decision. I'm not saying you don't need to do this, because you do. It just doesn't help you develop your idea. After an entrepreneur listens to the mindset training, the motivational content, some online "business gurus", and a talk from Oprah, they are still left sitting in the starting block with an idea and NO direction. Even if an entrepreneur stumbles up on things like Lean Start-Up methodology or Design Thinking methodology (which are both awesome by the way) there is still confusion on the practical steps needed to get out of the gate.

Vision to Value will give you a step by step, even inch by inch method for building a foundation your business can stand on top of. Once you get it you can use it over and over again for all of your ideas. The principles in the Vision to Value framework never change. After you read this book you really can just rinse and repeat the steps for the rest of your entrepreneurial career. This book is not meant to replace any of the other business content available. It will actually enhance all the other stuff by giving entrepreneurs some structure. Everything else an entrepreneur reads will make a lot more sense after reading this book. I will show you what to do today to launch your idea. I will give you the exact steps to take right now. I will give you concrete tools for a clear direction. This book will be the difference between your business failing and having a chance to make it to the next level.

Who is this book for?

This book is for anyone in business starting with the entrepreneur. Entrepreneurs will get a clear roadmap for how to approach and develop an idea. They will **finally** have a blueprint for what to do today with their ideas; these are true next steps. When you search "how to start a business" on Google or Youtube, the information you get isn't very helpful. You see hundreds of videos literally telling people to "analyze the competition" or "register your business with the state", or my favorite, "build your social media following." Not saying this information is all bad, but entrepreneurs need to know what they need to do today to push their ideas forward, and **none of these things are helpful to an entrepreneur that does not know where to start**. People think if it's on YouTube and published by someone who has a lot of followers, it is legit. But looks can be deceiving. Example: I saw someone on YouTube who gave a five-step guide on starting a business. Here are the steps in all of their glory:

1. Have an idea
2. Register with the state
3. Research the competition
4. Write a business plan
5. Marketing and social media

This is horrible advice for a new entrepreneur or struggling business owner that needs to know what to do next. But this video got 35K views (SMH). There were hundreds more videos and articles that follow the same trend of thought. Any entrepreneur out there that is wondering if this kind of information is legit, I have the answer. The answer is not even close.

The misinformation that is easily available to entrepreneurs today contributes to why businesses are failing at such a high rate. The mainstream information out there is pushing people to focus on studying competition and building a social media following, instead of the things that really matter. This book was created specifically to help and save businesses from failing and to give clear direction to people who want to start businesses or side hustles. Sometime entrepreneurs need to start a business because of market conditions (lost job, no money, or not enough money, etc.) This book is a quick and easy to read business blueprint any entrepreneur or existing business owner can use immediately for their business or idea. My blueprint is based in business strategy. It's real business stuff for real entrepreneurs, the stuff you don't see often in the mainstream media environment.

There are a few other groups of people who will find immediate value from reading this book: all of my business coaches or consultants out there! You should have your clients read this book. It will help you be more successful with delivering your content and programming. The Vision to Value framework will give your people the basic framework that everything else in business builds on. For example, if you specialize in branding, marketing, operations, HR, etc., your clients will understand your concepts much more clearly after they have read this book.

If you are in leadership at an existing company, this book will give your employees an easy framework for understanding your business, which in turn will assist them in understand how they fit in. This will help with things like on-boarding, team building and innovation planning. Today, all businesses have a need for their employees to think entrepreneurially. This can be difficult for people who work at companies, because they are not entrepreneurs. This book gives any employee a basic framework to start with. Vision to Value increases the employee's capacity to think outside of the box. Everyone can create, some people simply need guidance on how to do it constructively. If you are leading a team and want to get your team or department aligned around an idea, new product or new service, this book is a great starting point and discussion queue for how to efficiently move forward. Everyone will be speaking the same language and have a basic understanding of who you are targeting and what value you are bringing to that group of people.

If you are a lender or investor in entrepreneurs, early stage companies, and small businesses, Vision to Value is a great risk mitigation tool. The businesses you invest in are much more likely to succeed if they understand my basic framework. Vision to Value should be a part of the underwriting process before any funding decision is made. It will give an important reassurance that a company at least understands the fundamental principles needed to execute their plan. This also will put investor and lender on the same page as when speaking about the potential opportunity. Most lenders still require the unabridged 40-page business plan that many entrepreneurs simply hire someone to write. These long and somewhat outdated documents can rarely be fully explained by the entrepreneur because it's more of a box that needs to be checked for funding. My goal is that every entrepreneur has the basic tools to understand and explain the key elements of their business. Vision to Value then becomes a much more streamlined framework that both the entrepreneur and the lender can align with to maximize the relationship potential.

As you can see, this book creates value on multiple sides of the table because every stakeholder will have a clear point of reference from the beginning. Everyone will speak the same language and ultimately be in sync on all the things that matter for business success. Having a clear and agreed upon starting point increases the odds of success dramatically; because the foundation on which everything else stands is solid. Science tells us that speed is how fast you go from point A to point B. Velocity on the other hand, is defined as speed in a certain direction. So what am I saying here? It's ok to be fast, but being fast **in a certain direction** is how to be most effective. I view business the same way. People have millions of ideas moving all over the world every day. The ideas that can get clear business direction are the ones that have a chance to truly come to life.

Why Did I Write This Book?

The very first reason why I wrote this book is my own personal experience. I have started multiple businesses and invested in multiple businesses over the last 20 years. I have not only studied core business principles, I've had to learn them from actual experience. This age-old statement certainly applies to me: I wish I would have known then what I know now. I've had some tremendous successes but also some tremendous failures as well. At this stage in my career, I am passionate about showing others the things it took me years to learn. The goal is to help people understand high-level business principles in a simplified, yet impactful way. People should not have to get an MBA from Stanford University to understand basic business concepts.

I have done business with many highly successful people over the years and they all have specific things they do to be successful in their businesses. What I noticed is that we all say the same thing in a bunch of different ways. However, the core principles remain the same. The success story around those principles is what gets personalized to each successful individual. This makes it difficult for the average person to decipher which action items they need to implement to move their ideas forward. Vision to Value offers a more generalized solutions that anyone can follow and implement. The difference between success and failure is sometimes a razor thin line. A few bad decisions from an entrepreneur too early in the business, could be a disaster. Vision to Value helps to bridge that gap, by showing entrepreneurs exactly what they need to do to be successful.

The last reason I wrote this book is because of the infamous Google search, "How do I start a business?" There is so much information (and misinformation) out there, that makes it very difficult to determine what's good and what's bad. State and federal websites focus on things like business formation and explaining the different business entities. There are also all types of videos and information about the many areas of the value chain (which we will discuss later) right at your fingertips. The main problem is understanding where a person should start. Additionally, there is tons of bad information and scams out there that make it even more difficult to find the information you really need. One of the most frustrating things, for entrepreneurs especially, is that they don't know what they don't know. They generally know they need help, but they don't know what help they need or where to find it. Trying to create business out of thin air is already a very challenging feat. Knowing that you need some help but not knowing what those things are is absolute torture for an entrepreneur. I know because I have been there. Early on in my career I literally said, "I wish someone would just tell me what to do next". I had a great idea but zero guidance on where to start.

What This Book is Not

This book is not motivation or mindset training. This is not meant to simply inspire and encourage. I'm not here to tell you to visualize your dreams and tomorrow they will come to you. This is not a book on marketing or on things like how to grow your social media following. We will not be discussing branding or business entities.

Even though sales cures just about every business ailment, this is not a book on sales. I'm not saying these things aren't very important, because they are. These just are not core principles to business success. If you start developing your ideas with any of those things, you will make things very difficult for yourself. However, doing any of the above things after you have read this book will make them 100 times more effective because you will have a clear direction on where they fit in. The Vision to Value framework gets down to the core fundamentals by which all the other areas are built. This book will bridge the gap between inspiration and execution. It will give a true road map for bringing business ideas to fruition no matter the business area or environment.

CHAPTER 2:

The Two Key Pieces

The Why

The biggest question that any successful business answers is "why." I know that may sound simple, but the question of "why" may be the single most important question of any business. Why do you do what you do? Why does your business exist? Why do your customers like and buy your products? Why do employees want to work for you? Why do investors want to invest in you? Why do customers tell their friends and family about your business? This question is consistently at the forefront of any business whether they know it or not. The businesses that can answer the "why" question effectively become the most successful businesses. The world-famous business and leadership authority, Simon Sinek, wrote a book entitled *Start with Why*. It is a great book that I would certainly recommend. However, the importance and validity of what people need to consider is encapsulated right in the title of the book. Everything in business starts with the why. The good thing about understanding the concept of "why" is that it is transferable to all areas of business. This is why the Vision to Value framework is so effective. Vision to Value uses the concept of "why" to build the foundation for your ideas or business. Once you put the "why" at the core of your business strategy, you become impactful no matter what your idea or business is. So as the title of Simon Sinek's book says, we are going to start with the why.

Vision to Value breaks the "why" down into two distinct parts: the external why and the internal why. These two elements are the centerpiece of all successful businesses no matter the size; from Amazon to Walmart to your local car wash or laundromat. There are so many stakeholders that have to be accounted for when considering how to move your idea forward. **Stakeholders are basically anybody that has an impact or are impacted by a business.** Stakeholders are the entire ecosystem of people that make up a business. The External Why represents the different "why's" of all those who engage your business from the outside. That would be groups like your customers, your strategic partners and your distributors. The Internal Why consist of the "why's" of those who are inside your business. This would be people like you yourself, your management team, your employees, your investors or your board.

Understanding that everything in business begins with the "why" for all of your stakeholders, is fundamental for the success of your ideas or business. Getting down to this basic level of assessment is a key driver of the process. Everything ties back to either the internal or external why; yes everything! Every problem that a business encounters has to do with either or both sides of the "why." When a business has a problem, it's because it has stopped adequately answering the question of "why" for one or more groups of its stakeholders. This understanding makes developing and assessing the business much more streamlined. Start with this simple understanding and you will be moving in the right direction out of the starting gate. You literally have to start with the basic question of "why" to know where to start with your ideas.

Vince Lombardi was one of the greatest NFL football coaches of all times. He coached the Green Bay Packers to multiple Superbowls. He was famous for how he used to start his preseason training camps. He would hold up a football and say, "Gentleman, this is a football." The lesson Coach Lombardi was teaching is that you have to get back to the basics before you do anything else. Football is very complex. There are hundreds of people that have to perform thousands of coordinated movements successfully in order to win. But before any of that is possible you have to understand the basics. The "why" is the basics of business. All the thousands of coordinated actions your business must do to be successful start with the "why." So, in the words of the great Vince Lombardi, ladies and gentlemen reading this book, this is a football.

Key take away: the "why" for any business breaks down into two parts: the external why and the internal why. The external why is all about the why for those who engage with your business from outside, like your customers. The internal why deals with the why for those who engage with your company from within, like you and your employees. External why figures out why someone would buy your product or services, while the internal why figures out why someone would work for you or invest in you. That's it. Those are the two parts to any business. As you will learn about me, I like to keep it simple, and understanding that all business breaks down into two parts makes it super easy to begin developing your idea or your business. If you have an existing business, this is especially helpful because you will quickly be able to find your footing and troubleshoot any issues you are having.

External Why

The external why is the most important part of your business because your business literally cannot exist without it. The external why focuses mainly on one particular group of your stakeholders. I'll give you a second to guess which group that is. Did you say your customers? If you did, you would be correct. A business without customers is not a business at all; it's more of a hobby. There is nothing wrong with a hobby, but you definitely need customers to be considered a business. The first part of the Vision to Value framework will show you step by step how to establish the why for your customers. A compelling why for your customers is the cornerstone of any business. Your external why will keep customers coming back over and over again to your business. Your external why is the very first and most important step for building the bridge to success. With this in place, you can also get investors, partners, board members and any other groups of external stakeholders to work with you. Even doing sales for your company becomes much, much easier if you have a great external why.

I have taught, trained and coached hundreds of entrepreneurs over the years. You would be surprised at how many are trying to figure out why they can't get investors or why their marketing efforts are not working. The first thing I do is take them back to the basics. I go directly to the external why for the customers they are trying to serve. Most of the times this gets straight to the root of an issue. You can't have a marketing campaign without having a compelling "why" for customers to engage with your business. Otherwise you are trying to market a business that can't get customers. Not a recipe for success. This is also the reason you never start with marketing when launching a business (take social media out of your mind for now). Investors will not invest in a company that doesn't know who their customers are and how to engage them. This is the reason the external why for your customers is always going to be step one, and THE most important thing you do.

I hear you asking me out there, what are the other steps for the external why? Great question. The external why consists of three parts: the value proposition, the value chain, and the business model. The value proposition breaks down who your customers are and why they buy from you. The value chain is all the things you do behind the scenes to deliver your product or service to your customer. The business model is the actual mechanism you use to exchange money for products or services with your customers. All business comes down to these three things. That's the reason I began this section by saying your external why is the most important part of your business. It is truly the life blood of your business. I have coached over a hundred businesses both large and small, and the core principles that drive them are in these three areas of the external why. If there is a problem with the business you can generally find it in the value proposition, somewhere in the value chain, or in the business model. When starting a business, these are the areas that must be completely developed before you move on to anything else.

The Internal why

The most important thing to understand about the internal why is that it gives you focus. Your internal why is the guiding light to the path forward. Let's be clear, your internal why is not some mystical magical thing. And even though it's based on your personal convictions, it is a solid and concrete building block for your business. The internal why is just as concrete as the external why. The external is the blueprint of how to get and keep customers, while your internal why gives the overall direction of the company. It's a very intimate dance that the external and internal why have to do for your business to be successful. You can get customers with a great external why, but what good is it to have customers if the company itself has no direction. Eventually the customers will want to leave. Think about this: you own a cruise ship and you get thousands of people on your boat because of an awesome external why. But the first question the people will ask once they are onboard is "where are we going?". If you can't tell people where you are going, they will want to get off of your boat. That is the power of the internal why. **The external why is what attracts people to your business, but the internal why is why they stay.** Consumers these days want to know that the companies they buy from are going in a positive direction. The narrative around why the company exists is just as important as the product or service it sells. The reason the internal why is based on personal convictions is because you are the only one who can tell your own story.

Now let's think in practical terms. The internal why gives your business direction, which we just discussed; but it also gives your business focus. Why is focus so important? Great question. Having a clear focus about what to do is an invaluable asset as a business owner. Entrepreneurs have to make hundreds of business decisions throughout the course of a week. The internal why gives you a path through the jungle of decisions that is constantly trying to swallow you up. The internal why will show you clearly things like who the right partners, investors, and employees are. People who align with your internal why will want to work for your business and invest in your business. Customers who align with your internal why will continue to come back, and they will tell their friends about your business. The reason is that there should be synergy between what is important to the business, and what is important to its people. That connection is what will make people go out of their way to make your business successful.

The internal why will show you clearly who to connect with and work with. It will also show you who not to connect with. I actually think that part is more important. Knowing what not to do is a great thing to understand in your business. The internal why certainly helps with that. Knowing who to walk away from in business is a powerful thing. This is especially true for entrepreneurs of companies in their early stages. When you are in the early stages, resources are limited. Generally, you don't have the bandwidth to waste any time or money on things that won't immediately help you build. The wrong partnership, investor or employee can literally suck the life out of a company. Larger companies could potentially weather this kind of misalignment, but smaller companies could actually go out of business. We will discuss alignment more a little later. The main thing to know right now is that the internal why will guide your business by giving you clear direction and focus.

How They Work Together

As I mentioned, the external why and the internal why are the two key pieces of any business. While this is true for all businesses, the connection between the two is where the power lies. When both of those pieces are working together in harmony, it creates a true competitive advantage for the business. The most successful businesses are bringing customers in with a great external why and keeping them because of a strong internal why. The alignment of the two areas makes sure that a business will continue to be successful into the future. If your customers, employees, investors, etc., buy into your overall direction, you could have them for life.

The importance of this type of alignment cannot be overstated. There are major corporations that have gotten caught in major negative PR situations because they somehow got misaligned with the overall vision of the company. When a business stops letting the internal why drive their decisions it is very difficult to recover. The reason is because the customers may love your products, but they also love why you do what you do (internal why). This is why a customer will not only buy from you, but they will also tell their neighbors about you as well. Or insist that their whole family switches over to your service. This loyalty is based largely on the connection you make with customers around your internal why. A customer may love your products, but it may be your commitment to excellent customer service, for example, that makes them continue to come back time and time again.

CHAPTER 3:

Value Proposition

What Is Value Proposition

Let's lay the first brick toward building your business empire. As mentioned, we will start with the external why for your customers. To do this we will examine a term that, I promise you, is **the most important part of your business**. All successful businesses from Amazon to your local car wash have mastered this one thing. I teach MBAs and students from multiple disciplines on the university level. I also consult with companies and organizations in multiple industries on business strategy. This foundational element of business is often overlooked and is certainly not presented in the mainstream entrepreneurial content that people are regularly consuming. This all important and fundamental component is called the "Value Proposition." The value proposition is the why for your customers. Everything in your business builds on top of a strong value proposition.

Having a strong value proposition is the basis for which almost all of your business decisions will be made. So, take your time in this section and read it again if necessary. Everything else you do in your business will be stacked on top.

Value proposition answers that question of "why" for your customers. What value are you bringing to your customers that makes your company the right one to fulfill the particular need they have at the moment? Are you confused? I can see your face pinched up like my students that I teach this stuff to. But stay with me, it's really easy. Let me explain. All customers have needs. You yourself are a customer of some kind. You have different needs all day. Whether it's being hungry and wanting to get lunch, or needing to buy a coat because it's getting cold outside.

All businesses do all day is satisfy the different needs of people, like you, at a profit. And I say "at a profit" because any business that satisfies a need without making money WILL go out of business (we will discuss this later). Value proposition is the reason why the customer chose your business out of the tens, hundreds or sometimes thousands of other businesses that could also satisfy that need. If you think about yourself, it is the reason why you picked the place you went for lunch today or why you picked the store you chose to buy your winter coat.

No business gets the customers they have by magic or luck. They have mastered their value proposition. They have designed and engineered their business to answer the why for their customers. Remember this fact (because it will come up again throughout the book), **the most successful businesses solve a specific problem for a specific group of people.**

'Value proposition is the reason why you may choose Chick-fil-A over McDonald's, Nike over Adidas, Coke over Pepsi, to fly on Delta over JetBlue. I could go on all night. The value proposition covers any and everything as it relates to understanding why a customer chooses the product or service that they choose. This understanding is an absolute key to being successful in business.

There is No Best

Harvard University Professor Michael Porter gives a great thought experiment to illustrate this foundational point. It's a very short exercise but very effective in showing value proposition. I want you to get one or two people with you (although it could be as many as you want) to do this exercise. This works well in small groups, for those who want to engage your leadership team. It also works well for team leads at a company working on a new innovation or idea. But even if it is just you are reading this book by yourself in the middle of the night, you can still easily think through the exercise.

I am going to ask you a series of 10 questions, and you answer them as honestly as you can. If you are leading this exercise with a group, you can make the series of questions as long as you want and with any theme that you choose.

1. What is the best car?
2. What is the best toothpaste?
3. What is the best shoe company?
4. What is the best fast food restaurant?
5. What is the best grocery store?
6. What is the best clothing brand?
7. What is the best cellphone?
8. What is the best place to vacation?
9. Who has the best pizza?
10. What is the best social media platform?

Did you notice anything about the answers you gave or were given by the group? The answers were likely very different from person to person. And some of the questions may have even evoked a more spirited response from the group, like the cellphone question. I always throw that one in for fun because there is bound to be the Android vs iPhone debate. You know the iPhone people will fight you over their iPhone's superiority (as I type this on my Mac, but I promise I'm not like that). All of the questions are somewhat subjective in nature. This means that everyone will have their own opinion.

So what does this have to do with business? The point of this exercise is to show you that **there is no best company in any category of business.** I'll repeat. There is no best company in any category of business. The key takeaway is that every person's answer was the best choice for them. The answer they gave satisfied their particular need better than other businesses in that space. If you did the exercise on your own, you answered the questions based on what works best for you. Remember that the best businesses solve a specific problem for a specific group of people.

Now let's go a little deeper. Let's break down the first question, *what is the best car?* Some people may say a Honda Civic. Some may say a Toyota RAV4. When I do this exercise with college students, they say things like a Range Rover or Lamborghini (it's funny how things change when you get older). Of course, we know that there really is no right answer. If you are a soccer mom or dad with three children, the Lamborghini is probably not the best option. That person probably named a car with third row seating, or maybe a minivan. If you are a single male with a very high level of disposable income, and you like to be flashy; the Lamborghini might be the right call. The point here is that the best option in any category **does not exist**. As a business, you want to be the best option for your particular customers.

Lamborghini would not be upset if the soccer dad complained to the company because there's no model that has third row seating and extra trunk space. On the other hand, the minivan dealer is not worried about the complaint that says their vans don't do 0-60 in two seconds and the doors don't fly up like eagle wings. The reason is because Lamborghinis are not made for soccer dads. That is not their particular customer. Lamborghini wants to be the best choice for the person who has 300K to spend and likes speed and flash. Lamborghini has a very clear value proposition.

Breaking down the Value Proposition

At this point you should begin seeing the importance of the value proposition. It pushes you to do the work to discover who "your" customers are. You don't just want customers, you want **your** customers. You want people who feel like your business is the best choice for them. But how do you do this? What if I told you there was a systematic 3 step formula for crafting your value proposition? Well today is your lucky day, because there is. Working through these three steps will give you a great value proposition that you can build everything else on top of.

The three steps are actually three questions every business must be able to answer. At first the questions sound simple; but putting them together in a way that makes sense is where the challenge lies. These three questions are the launching point no matter the size or age of your business. If you have an idea you want to bring to market or you are an established company looking to add a new product or service to your line up; this is the place to start.

- Question 1. Who is your target customer?
- Question 2. What problem are you solving for them?
- Question 3. How much do you charge them?

These three questions make up the value proposition. Again, I know it sounds basic, but putting these three things together in a meaningful way is the center of any business success. Every business answers these three questions differently. This is why the secret sauce is all in how you put the pieces together. The questions themselves are all the same for each business. The answers, however, will be as different as night and day, even for businesses in the same industry. We will talk through a few examples at the end of this section so you can see the value proposition at work. You will also be able to see clearly the importance of having a value proposition that makes sense.

Question 1: Who is your target Customer?

This question is self-explanatory but the reasoning behind why it is significant makes all the difference. As we've discussed, value proposition is one of the most important parts of any business. When I meet clients for any type of strategy development, I start with the company's value proposition. And the first question of the value proposition is about the target customer. In talking to company owners over the years, the first thing I ask them is who is your target customer. You would be surprised at how many business owners cannot identify who their target customer is. Many entrepreneurs work under the idea that anyone who will buy their stuff is a target customer. This idea is extremely far from the truth and ultimately leads businesses into the graveyard.

Knowing your target customer is a must if you are going to find "your people;" the ones who think your business is the best choice for them. **It is much better to be the best solution for 50 people than an average solution for 500 people.** This is why knowing who your customers are, is such an important piece of the puzzle.

Knowing your target customer also gives you focus. You will know exactly who it is you are serving. Focus is pivotal in delivering maximum value to your customer. So now you can focus all your resources on one particular group of people. Just think, what if you only had a limited budget to do something like marketing and advertising? Working with a limited budget is almost always the case when you have a startup or an early stage company. $5,000 for instance, goes much further on social media if you know the group of people you want to target.

If you don't have a target customer group something would break down very quickly; because it can get extremely expensive to market to everyone. But if your target customers are minority black women between the ages of 18 and 30, you can use your limited resources much more effectively. Having a target customer will give you insights on things like where to find them or what platforms they frequent most. If you are targeting professionals, you may want to advertise on LinkedIn instead of TikTok. Knowing who your customer is gives you the direction and clarity you need when developing your value proposition and your overall plan.

Lamborghini knows exactly who their customer is. They know where to find that customer and how to market to that customer. The person who buys a Lamborghini loves that car. It is the right one for them. Remember it is better to be the best choice for a small amount of people than to be just an average choice for a lot of people. No one just accidentally buys a Lamborghini. It's a $400K car. Lamborghini would rather spend their time winning a customer who absolutely loves them, a happy lifelong customer.

Now let's looks at the other side of the coin. Knowing your target customer also gives you direction of what not to do. You don't hear much about this side of the game. But the success of your business is probably more determined by the things you don't do as a business owner than the things you do. I tell my clients all the time that the best business strategies are going to make some people upset, and that's ok. This idea of making everyone happy as a business is complete garbage. I hate to be so blunt, but it's true. Once you know the customers you are targeting, everything you do should be to address and improve their experience with you.

Let's go back to the example from earlier when the soccer dad complains to Lamborghini about third row seating and trunk space. You won't ever see Lamborghini try to make a minivan to make that customer happy. Lamborghini is alright that the soccer dad is upset with their cars, because he is not their target customer. Knowing who you are not trying to service is very empowering. It takes you out of the middle of the road and away from the indifferent place that a lot of businesses get caught in. Remember that people choose to engage with companies that are the best for them and their needs. If your business is neither bad nor good to them, they will never choose you.

Having clarity on who your customer is will change the game for you as an entrepreneur, or in a company as the leader of a team working on a new product or service. If you are an established business owner and you want to expand business, this is always the place to start. "Who is your customer?" is a fundamental driver for taking any business concept and moving it in the right direction. Think about your business, no matter where you are in the business life cycle. Can you clearly articulate who your customer is? Is it men, women, children, veterans, minorities, homeless, affluent people, other businesses like yours? Who is it? Begin to think about the people you would like to serve with your business. The better you get at identifying that person, the clearer their profile will start being in your mind. You should almost be able to see them and imagine them shopping for your products or using your service.

Now that you understand the importance of naming your target customer, let me assure you that it doesn't have to end there. Many entrepreneurs ask me if they can ever go after the other customers they think they can engage. The answer is a resounding yes, but this is where you start. You have to pick a group and be the best for them. Then you can consider expanding to other customer groups that make sense. The Vision to Value framework is made to give any businessperson pursuing something new a place to start today. You can immediately put this framework into practice in any business. When you are ready to expand, you can take this process and start again using your new potential target customers. It's that simple.

Think about Amazon. I would think that everyone reading this book has heard of this company. They started in the nineties selling schoolbooks and other difficult to find books. It was a very specific group of customers they were targeting at first. I bought a few textbooks from them back when I was in school. Today, 25 years later, they sell just about anything to anybody. They started with people that needed books, then they gradually expanded from there. So the thing I want you to really take in is that you have to choose up front who you are going to serve. As the old saying goes, you need to pick a horse and ride it!

Question 2. What problem are you solving for them?

Now that you have picked a target customer, you have to figure out what problem you are going to solve for them. To do this we will examine three terms that will help you bring this question into focus. First thing you need to understand is that businesses that don't solve problems quickly go out of business, and rightfully so. The best businesses solve a specific problem for a specific group of people. You now know the specific group of people. Now you must discover what problem your business is going to solve for them. What are you going to do that will make your business the best choice for your target customer group?

To discover this, I am going to introduce our first term which is "pain points." Pain points are all the problems, deterrents or even irritations a person experiences with any sort of business engagement. When trying to find a problem to solve, you must start with the pain points. Think about the industry you are in or the industry you want to go into. Now think about how your target customer group fits into that industry. What problems, deterrents or irritations do you see "your people" having in this space? If you're opening a car wash, what problems are your target customers having at other car washes in the area? Are the lines too long? Is it too expensive? Maybe your target customers are high-end car owners and they like their cars hand washed. Maybe there aren't any other hand wash car washes in the local area.

One thing you can do is see if you yourself fit into your target customer group. Then you can consider what problem you may have in the industry you want to do business in. If your target customer for your car wash is high-end car owners, but you don't own a Bentley or a Porsche, you can't think about what pain points you have, because you don't represent your target customer. However, if you're opening a regular car wash and you drive a regular car, then your pain points are valid.

Now let's apply this framework to any business space you are in or entering. Think of your target customers. Then consider what their pain points are. Graphic arts, t-shirt printing, hair stylist, restaurants, app development, you can apply this to anything. What pain points are your customers experiencing with any industry?

Next, make a list of the pain points that you see your target customers having with the industry you are in. Everything matters at this stage of the process. Nothing is too small to consider. Get as specific as you can. The reason is, by digging deep you may uncover something that is really meaningful to your target customer and is not being addressed elsewhere. Finding these pain points are what make customers love a company. Think again about Amazon. They went to "one-click" payment options because they saw a pain point. Their customers hated having to click through so many times to purchase their items. This pain point basically translates into the problem of losing business because the checkout process was too long. From that pain point Amazon revamped their whole payment system to streamline the entire purchasing experience down to one click. Talk about going deep on your customers pain points. Two clicks are too many! But this type of example is why Amazon is the best choice for so many people.

The second term I am going to introduce as we understand that the problem we are solving is "customer insights." Customer insights are the things that make your target customers unique for the business space you are in. After you have made a list of pain points your target group of customers are experiencing, what insights can you gather about your people? Gather your insights from understanding your pain points. What can you learn about your target customers by examining their pain points? You may learn that women are the target customer, but men are the ones who actually pay for the product or service. Think about a business that sells roses or mobile spa treatments. Think about a toy business. You may say that kids are your target customers, but one key insight is that an adult has to actually pay for the product. No matter how much the child wants your toy, kids don't have credit cards. Maybe your target customers are women between the age of 25 and 40. And after you examine their pain points, you notice that some of them have a child or children with them at the time of purchase. It can be frustrating trying to navigate a transaction with a child demanding your attention. That is an insight. Insights are small but significant things you can learn about the people you want to serve. Go through your list of pain points and see if you can pull out a few insights about your target customer group.

Don't think you're doomed if you can't find a bunch of insights at first. It may take a little time to really understand your people. This brings me to my last term that will help you discover what problem you will be solving with your business: customer development. This term was made popular by an absolute heavy weight in the entrepreneurial space, Steve Blank. There is a whole methodology behind his work that I would definitely suggest you explore. Today we are just going to talk about one small part of customer development that I teach because it is very helpful for this part of the value proposition.

So what is customer development? Customer development is the idea of the business owner engaging with their target group. In other words, get your butt out of the office and go talk to your target customers. After you have decided who your target customer is and begun working through pain points and insights, the best thing to do is to go talk to these people. You will be surprised about how effective some real-time conversation with your target customers can be. I have consulted with companies of all sizes and many of them have never considered just getting out of the office and talking to folks. This can be especially impactful if you are a new business trying to find what works. Larger more established companies already have customers, so they tend to want to skip this step. In either case there is no better feedback than that of your target customers. You may think that your customers are younger women, but discover after engaging that younger men are actually the ones who love what you are doing. This "insight" would fundamentally change everything. Targeting men not women takes a whole different thought process.

So what do you talk about with your target customers? That's easy. Talk about that pain points and insights you have discovered throughout this process. They will be able to tell you which pain points are most important to them (which is an insight). They will also be able to tell you why it would be important for your business to address that pain point. Remember "the why" from the beginning of the book. This section goes to the heart of the external why. The why for your customers. Why did they choose you? These interactions with your customers will really help you to understand their why.

You may be saying that you are not a people person, that you can't go out to talk to people. Don't worry, that is actually a common reaction from people. My advice is either swallow that anxiety and do it anyway or partner with someone who is good at it. Someone has to be able to get consistent feedback from your people. Notice I said consistent. The customer development process doesn't stop once we finish locking in your value proposition. The most successful businesses are always talking to the people they serve to make sure that they remain the best choice for them. I know this step may be intense, but it will be all worth it when your customers keep coming back to your business.

Now let's put it all together. By now you should have a list of pain points and insights. You should also have some feedback from your actual customers. Take all of this information and pick one or two, maybe three of the largest issues you have discovered throughout this process. Make those the key problems that you are going to solve with your new business or new product or service. Don't try to solve every problem you discover. Direct your attention, efforts, and resources to a few key areas that mean the most to your people. And get specific. This way it will be easy to identify and explain what you are doing.

You should now be able to clearly articulate who your customer is, and what problem you are solving for them. We are on our way. We only have one more question to tackle to get our value proposition completely locked in.

Question 3. What Do You Charge Your Customers?

This question is the icing on this value proposition cake we are baking. We will discuss two terms in this section to help you determine how much you charge your customers. But before we go deeper, you must understand that the answer to this question is not going to be an actual number. It's more of a place on the price spectrum. Let's go back to our car example from earlier. Think Honda and think Lamborghini. Are you going to price your products or services on the high end or on the low end of the price spectrum? Do see your business as a Lamborghini or as more of a Honda? Please don't think that it's better or worse to be either, because both car companies are very successful. Each just has a different target customer group. Do you have high end clientele? Are your clients everyday working people? Maybe your clients depend on social services. **When you look at your industry, where do you want to fit?** The key idea is that you have to pick which pricing area you want to be in. The last thing to remember before we get into our terms, is that this decision is totally up to you. This is your business, so you choose where you want to be on the spectrum. The only thing you have to be sure of is that your pricing area aligns with the first two parts on the value proposition. **The value proposition only makes sense if all three parts work in harmony together.** Here is a quick example. If you decided, from question one, that your target customers are more resource constrained and are looking for cheaper options, you probably should not price your products on the higher end of the price spectrum. The opposite also works. If you want your clients to be rich, more affluent people, you can't price your products on the low end of the price spectrum; because those people pay for luxury and quality. If you have a counseling practice that charges clients out of pocket $400 per hour, your office cannot be in a bad part of town. All the pieces of your value proposition have to work together.

Let's examine the two terms that will help you bring it all together. The first term is "differentiation," and the second term is "low cost." Pop quiz: if you think about the car example from above (Honda vs. Lamborghini), can you guess which term represents the high end of the price spectrum, and which represents the low end? We will discuss this further in a minute, but "differentiation" represents the higher end, and "low cost" represents the lower end. Did you guess correctly?

Differentiation means that your product or service has something unique about it that will allow you to charge more. Low cost means that your product may not have anything super unique about it, which allows you to charge lower more affordable prices. These are the two fundamental categories that 99% of businesses will fit into. Your business is going to be either, not both. You have to decide here and now what area you are going to play in. Now let's get a little deeper.

There are thousands of examples that I can think of, that shows these two terms in action. Here are a few everyday brands you can consider as examples:

- Walmart vs Target
- Apple vs Android
- McDonalds vs Ruth's Chris Steak House
- Honda vs Lamborghini
- Neiman Marcus vs Macy's
- Red Bottoms vs Nine West
- Whole Foods vs Safeway
- Givenchy vs Gap

I could go on and on. Just about everyone has been to a Walmart or knows what Walmart is. They are known as the cheapest in town. Walmart operates in the low-cost category. If want the cheapest price, you think Walmart. On the other hand, if you feel like you want to step it up a bit and go for more quality, you think Target. Target would be considered differentiated. Target has said that they are not going to try to beat Walmart at being the cheapest in town. They decided to charge more for their products, but you get higher quality and a better store experience. Remember that both ends of the price spectrum work just fine. Walmart and Target are both very successful. The key for you as an entrepreneur is deciding which area you want to be. If you are an employee working for a company or leading a team, knowing where your company stands is fundamental to understanding how to move things forward in your area. Can you think of any other differentiated vs. low cost examples? They are all around us every day. If you can't think of any right now, you will recognize many examples just by the experiences you have in your daily life. The more you see this part of the value proposition in action, the better you will understand what's best for your business.

Differentiation

Differentiation is generally what brings you into the higher end of the price spectrum. Is there anything that is unique about your business that would make your customers pay more? Do you use higher quality materials? Do you maybe have a patent that will prevent others from copying you? Are you the only company who can provide a certain service to the community? Does your clothing company maybe hand-stitch or custom make orders? These are all things that would allow you to charge more for your products and services. Differentiation is all about uniqueness and standing out in a way that is special from others in the space.

How do you know if your products or services are differentiated? How do you know your target customer would pay more? Remember that each element of the value proposition builds off of one another. All three pieces must be in sync to work properly. I say this because you will know very clearly whether your customers would pay more if you took the time to get deep on the first two parts of the value proposition. You would have seen some insights and had some conversations that would indicate that your customers would pay more. If you have a differentiated service that caters to people who have money, then you can charge more for the service. But the first two parts of the value proposition make that possible. The bottom line is that your customer will tell you directly or indirectly if they would pay more. If you launch an expensive and differentiated product that nobody wants or buys, that means you need to go back to step one or two of the value proposition. Either you have the wrong group of people or you are not solving the right problem for them. Or maybe both.

Your business will undoubtedly have to decide which end of the price spectrum to participate in. Many entrepreneurs shy away from the differentiated higher end area because they lack the creativity to think outside of the box. Being unique definitely takes creativity. So instead of building that skillset or partnering with someone who has it, entrepreneurs automatically go for low cost. Or even worse, they get stuck in the middle, a no man's land where companies go to die (more on this later).

It may sound intimidating, but everyone can be creative and think outside of the box. And if that truly is not you, consider bringing in a creative person before you automatically shift away from differentiation. Maybe you could get a start-up coach to assist with looking at different angles of your business. Let's say you have a hotdog stand downtown in your city; and every other stand in the area sells their hotdogs for $1. Are you going to get into the very competitive $1 hotdog game? Or can you sell $4, fresh, beef or pork sausages sourced from local farms. It's a slight variation on the current hotdog game you are in, but with better, more healthier products you can charge more money for. And by the way, you will know this is a good option because the people who buy the $1 hotdogs everyday have told you in step one and two of the value proposition, that they would pay a little more for a healthier, better tasting option. Remember, the more work you do in each step of the value proposition, the clearer your options will be as you go to market.

Differentiation is a bold way to consider where you think your business should be. Don't assume that there isn't anything new and innovative you can do to be unique and set yourself apart. All areas of business are ripe for disruption. This means that there is always something different that can be done. Entrepreneurial-minded people can always find ways to the path of differentiation. If you're at a big company, apply this thinking to your current product lineup. You may surprise yourself (and your company).

Low-cost

The low-cost end of the price spectrum is a bit easier to unpack than differentiation. The reason is because you're basically just looking to be the cheapest price than others on the market. You aren't trying to give your customers unique products; you are strictly focused on giving them lower cost products. Think about the mass produced $100 Swatch watch, versus the $10,000 hand crafted Rolex watch. When you decide to take a low-cost approach for your customers, you are looking to give them the most value for a dollar that they can get. Therefore, you should be positioning yourself for a lot of people to buy your stuff. Let's look back at our Honda/Lamborghini comparison. Lamborghini's average price is around $200,000 per car. It's a very high price, but that's why they only sell about 10,000 cars per year. Honda, on the other hand, averages about $20K per car; and they sell about 5,000,000 cars per year.

There is nothing wrong with being low cost. You just have to really commit to it. One thing that is a recipe for disaster is starting out low cost but then changing your mind to be high end. This almost never works. Once you have established yourself as a low-cost provider for your customers, it is nearly impossible to get them to pay more. This is why you have to be careful when you decide to be a low-cost player. Once you decide, you're generally locked in.

Another thing to consider about being low cost is that it generally puts you in a race to zero. This is a business term which means that other companies will always find a way to be cheaper that you. Even though being low cost is easier to understand it is harder to maintain. Let's say you offer a $40 massage at the mall. You offer this price so your customers can get a decent massage at a low price. It will go well for a while, until someone next door comes out with the $35 massage that is just as good. If your main incentive to your customers is a low-cost massage, how will you keep your customers from going next door for the $35 option? Since everything is based on being low cost, the only way to keep your customers is to offer the $30 massage. Of course, now the guys next door have to do the same thing to keep up, and now introduce a $25 massage. This is what the race to zero looks like. This is why it is always better to find a way to be unique or differentiated. While everyone else is racing to zero with cheaper and cheaper massages, you would never have to change your price if you found a way to offer unique massages. Maybe you serve glasses of champagne with your massage or something.

The Wrap up

Now that you understand the difference between low cost and differentiation, you are ready to complete your value proposition. The value proposition solves a specific problem, for a specific group of people, at a certain price. This is literally the core of any and every business on the planet. Understanding the principle of value proposition is the baseline for anything you will do in business. This should be required knowledge for everyone in business, not just entrepreneurs. All employees need to have this understanding about their company in order to do their job more effectively. Even if your company is big and has multiple products and services, each one of them is solving a problem for a target customer group, at a certain price. Remember, the power of the value proposition for your business is in how you put the pieces together. The framework I've given you is pretty straight forward. But each of the millions of people who read this book will answer in his or her own special way.

I want you to think of some of your favorite companies. Can you clearly see their value proposition? If you shop there, why are those companies the best choice for you? The funny thing about value proposition is once you understand it you will be able to see it everywhere; whether it's your business or the businesses in your neighborhood. Anytime you see people in line purchasing something anywhere you can now examine why they chose that place. The value proposition tells the story. You can even examine the companies you see on TV. I am a fan of Elon Musk and SpaceX. He started SpaceX to be a "lower cost" provider of space services for governments and large private companies (his customer groups) who need to send things to space. SpaceX has a $100 Billion valuation, but you and I can still break down their value proposition in 5 minutes. This is why the value proposition is core to any business. It doesn't matter what you do or how big your business gets its all driven by a strong value proposition. Marketing, branding, sales, and every other part of business builds on top of the value proposition. Everything else in business will make a lot more since if you understand these principles first.

CHAPTER 4:

Value Chain

What is the Value Chain?

This section will start to bring some color to your business. By now you should have a good outline for what your business is going to look like. The value chain begins layering on top of that picture. So what is it? What is the value chain? The value chain is a composition of all the things you need to do, and choices you need to make, to bring value to your customers. It quite literally brings the value proposition to life. **It's the complete set of activities that you do to actually deliver your products or services to the target customer.** Think of the value chain as a machine. Stuff goes in at the beginning of the process. Then stuff comes out the other end ready to go to the customer. For the purposes of this discussion, we will keep it as simple as possible. There are whole books and courses on value chain alone, just like every other topic we've talked about. I would recommend every entrepreneur to read more about these topics after this book. I've mentioned it before, my aim is to give you the basics so you will know how to get started, and where to spend your time and resources.

The definition of business itself is simply selling a product or service for less than the cost to produce it. We started the external why discussion with the value proposition, so we could understand a basic outline for what you are trying to accomplish with your idea. This includes your target customers and your target price point. The value chain will give you a look at the complete process to produce your product or service. Remember what I just said, business is simply selling something for more than it took to produce it. The value chain will tell exactly how much it cost to produce your stuff. In the last part of the value proposition you decided where you wanted to be on the price spectrum. Your price target and your value chain are the two things you need to determine whether you fit into the basic definition of what a business is. Does your product or service cost less than what you decided to sell it for?

If you have an idea, and then start by working through the value proposition, you are on the right track. But then you may look at the value chain and realize that it's not possible to get your product produced at a lower price than you laid out in your value proposition. You would then have to go back and change something. In this scenario, you would either think about charging more for your stuff or seeing how you can get the cost lower in your value chain. It's as simple as that. This is true if you are an entrepreneur with a new idea, or if you work for an established company and have a new idea for your organization. This framework I'm giving you is made up of pieces that you can move around until you get the exact result you desire. This is your business and you can position it however you best see fit.

As you can see, the value chain goes hand and hand with the value proposition. One builds off the other to create a snapshot of what your business will ultimately look like. The value chain itself is made up of small individual pieces that add up to your total cost to produce your product or service. You will make individual choices in five key areas, which we will discuss in a minute. The decisions you make in each area will be different from the decisions someone else makes in these same key areas. Similar to the value proposition, the way you put the five pieces together is what determines a successful value chain. Even for businesses that are in the same industry as you, no two value chains will be alike. You can't just copy another business's value chain and think you will be successful. The thing that absolutely sets the winners apart from the losers is based on the decisions that are made in the value chain. This will equal a major advantage for you. You can win over your competitors simply because you have a better value chain. Remember that business is just selling for less than producing. The value chain is all about efficiency in making and delivering your product or service. If you can produce your product or service cheaper or more efficient than everybody else, you will consistently be on top.

So where do you start with your business? You should of course, have your value proposition dialed in. Next, make a list of all the things you need to bring your products and services to your customer. This is nothing but a good old-fashioned brainstorming session. You and your team could get a white board and just start writing all the things that come to your mind. We will move them into categories next; but I like to start with an unstructured brain dump, to get as much stuff on paper as possible. I also find that this activity gets the motor going for putting together a great value chain. This part does not have to be super long or formal. Just get some things down on paper. Now that you have your list, let's go a bit deeper.

The concept of the value chain was first introduced in the eighties by Harvard professor and economist, Michael Porter. Professor Porter is an international business authority. He said that all businesses on the planet have a set of activities that are common, called the value chain. He goes into a deep dive in his groundbreaking book *Competitive Advantage*. I would definitely suggest you read some of his materials.

Professor Porter breaks the value chain down into five key primary areas:

- Inbound logistics- The unfinished stuff or separate pieces that comes into your business to make your product or service, like raw materials.

- Operations- Any process of turning these pieces into final products.

- Outbound Logistics- Any process of delivering the final products or service to the customer, like postage or last-mile delivery services (FedEx, UPS, etc.).

- Marketing and Sales- Communicating your messaging to people and customers and selling the product or service.

- Service- All engagement with customers after they have bought stuff from you. This will include things like service and maintenance.

Professor Porter also discusses key support activities in his value chain model: infrastructure, human resources, technology, and procurement. These four areas support the five primary areas we just discussed. Many of the support activities are generally performed by the entrepreneur in early stage companies or small businesses. If anyone here has started a business before, you know that you have to wear many hats. Of course, if you have a larger company that has multiple departments, I would certainly recommend you review the support activities in the value chain. For the sake of the discussion in this book we will focus on the primary value chain areas. **Remember, the five primary value**

chain areas are present in every business on the planet, including yours. Whether you are starting a business or assessing how to improve an existing business, the value chain holds the key. The value chain is something every entrepreneur needs to spend time thinking about.

Before I go any further, I have to say something. Do not feel intimidated by all of this complicated university talk. All the value chain is, is a way to organize what goes in and what comes out. Whatever kind of business you have, there is something going in one end and stuff coming out the other. The value chain is that process. Even though the university talk is the official way to discuss the value chain, you can keep it very simple in your mind. After you have the value proposition, the value chain shows you all the stuff you will need to make it happen. That is it. Your value chain is your superpower as an entrepreneur. Because how you bring your value proposition to your people will be different from all the other businesses.

Even though the primary areas of the value chain are present in all businesses, not every area will weigh equally for every business. Make sure you carefully consider each area to see which primary areas will be focal points for you. Some businesses require a balance across each of the five primary value chain areas. If you are a product-based company, your value chain will probably touch each area, everything from getting the raw materials in, to servicing customers after they have received the product. But if you are an accountant and you run a tax business, inbound logistics and operations may not be as big for you. Marketing and service, however, are probably huge parts of your value chain because people will call you all year about their taxes after you have completed them. My sister owns her own mental health counseling practice. The value chain for her business is similar to the tax business. It is really heavy on marketing, sales and service. Her clients can call her any time after they have received their counseling session. She has had to organize her value chain to account for clients that may need her outside of the appointment times. This is the service part of the value chain. Let's say there is a competitor who also offers mental health counseling but does not offer service outside of appointment time. My sister's business would be more competitive to clients because the service part of her value chain is better than the competition. When it comes to true competitive advantage, the value chain is where all the action is.

Generally speaking, when entrepreneurs add up the costs of the five primary areas of the value chain, you understand overall how much it costs to produce your product or service. Remember, you want your cost to be lower than the price point you outlined in your value proposition. The lower you can get your cost relative to how much you charge your customers, the more money you will make. Sounds like pretty simple subtraction but many entrepreneurs never take the time to examine these elements. Then they wonder why they are not making any money. Or why investors aren't interested in giving them money. If you can barely get the cost of production below your selling price, there is no room for any investment.

You all probably already know this about me. I feel the best way to really share business principles is to walk through real-world examples together. Once you get the hang of it, it's easy to apply the value chain principles to your business. If you have followed the Vision to Value framework so far, this is just the next step in the process.

Let's apply these five primary areas to a t-shirt business. Because of social media, it's easier than ever to start a clothing brand. So how would the value chain look for a t-shirt business? At this point you would already have your value proposition locked in. Let say you have decided that your target customer is women under 30 years old who want stylish options but prefer comfort. The problem you're solving is that you provide stylish yet comfortable t-shirt options for young women who like to be cute but are always on the go, and there aren't many options that fit this category. You have also decided to stay on the lower, more economic end of the price spectrum. So, you will sell your t-shirts for $35. Now that you have a quick snapshot of the value proposition, let's look at the value chain.

First, we need to brainstorm. Make an initial list of all the things you would need to sell a t-shirt to a customer. Start by writing down the first things that come to your mind. Things like, social media (maybe Facebook and Instagram), ink, shirt heat press machines or screen printing machines, flyers, a website, etc. Make this list as long as you want. More things will come to mind as we separate them into the five areas of the value chain. You can skip the brainstorming step if you would prefer to go straight to the five areas of the value chain. Personally, I find it a little easier to approach the five areas after you have done a short brainstorming session. The brainstorming session gets you thinking outside the box. Now that you have your list, what would the value chain actually look like?

T-Shirt Inbound logistics

Inbound logistics are things like the ink and the blank t-shirts you will use to make your final product. These are the elements that would be considered inputs for your products. If you were baking a cake, for example, inbound logistics would cover things like eggs, milk, butter, cream, and chocolate frosting (I guess you can see the kind of cakes I like). Inbound logistics is basically just like it sounds. It's all the raw materials or unfinished pieces you need to make your product or to deliver your service. Remember your list from above. You should already have a good idea of what your raw material needs look like for the t-shirt business. Next you have to decide where you would be getting each piece from. Where are you going to get your blank t-shirts from?

What brand will you use? Can you get them cheaper if you buy wholesale?

Remember that everything we have done so far helps to shape your decisions. Everything is a building block that we are stacking on top of one another. Think about the value proposition for this t-shirt business, which we outlined above. We decided that we are selling our t-shirts at the moderate price of $35 dollars. When we are looking at inbound logistics, which is the first part of the value chain, we have to keep our value proposition in mind. Since we are selling our t-shirts for $35, can we get the most expensive blank t-shirts as part of our inbound logistics? The answer is probably not. But you probably don't want to get the absolute cheapest either. You could start by looking at all the companies that sell blank t-shirts; then consider the price and the quality. Maybe you can do a few small test orders from different companies to feel the quality for yourself. The key point is that you must be as thorough as possible in each step of the value chain because it will make a difference in the end. The price point of your blank t-shirts (raw material) ultimately plays a part in you beating the price point you laid out in your value proposition. Remember that each piece of the value chain will add up to the total cost to produce your product or service.

T-Shirt Operations

This step is about taking all the things you identified for inbound logistics and turning them into a finished product. Do you have some things on your list you can fit into this category? Operations is the process of taking your design, the ink and the blank t-shirt, putting them on a heat press machine and ending up with a completed t-shirt. You then will add your hang tag, fold or roll the t-shirt and place into your packaging. Now you have a completely finished product ready to go to a customer.

T-Shirt Outbound Logistics

This step is about taking that finished, packaged t-shirt and actually getting it into the customers hands. It's the process you use to get the finished, packaged t-shirt from your office to its destination. Does FedEx come by the office to pick up packages every day? Do you use Stamps.com for your postage? Do you drive to each customers house to deliver each t-shirt by hand? That may sound crazy but that could be how you want to do it. Of course, you would then have to factor in the cost of gas to drive to people's houses. Whatever your process would be to get the t-shirt from your office, warehouse, or garage to the customer is covered here.

T-Shirt Marketing and Sales

This part is where a lot of entrepreneurs start when they have an idea. They are looking at Facebook ads and Instagram business posts before they even have a solid value proposition. Most entrepreneurs don't realize that marketing and sales is part of a much bigger eco-system called the value chain. It's a small part in a bigger process, and each part of the process has to work together for you to be successful. Many entrepreneurs have never been told about the value chain, which puts them at a disadvantage. Now that you are here, how do you market and complete sales for your t-shirts? How are you going to get your messaging out there? Who is going to sell your shirts? Social media is one of the most obvious places these days because it's free and effective. How else would you get your messaging out about your t-shirts? I've heard of people just talking to everyone they see and selling their t-shirts out of the trunk of their cars, which is certainly a way to do it. There are plenty of resources available to help with putting together a great plan for marketing and sales. This is actually one of the areas of business that is very overdone. There are thousands of marketing "gurus" of there. You really just have to pick the best avenue for you to market and sell the t-shirts to your particular customers. The methods are endless, and the opportunities are infinite.

T-Shirt Service

This is simply your after-the-sell engagement. Things like returns would be involved in this step. What happens if someone's t-shirt is messed up? What process do you have for making things right with the customer? These are the types of things that covered in the service part of the value chain. What other engagements can you think of that might go on after a customer has purchased a t-shirt? T-shirt sales seem pretty straight forward but there could be other service-related issues. What if some orders a t-shirt and it never gets to them? What if the order they do get is the wrong order? As you can see, the service part of the value chain can be the difference between a customer ordering again or not at all.

Once you have resolved any issues and have successfully brought a customer through your value chain, you can now reassess how things are. This is something I always tell my students. The value chain is the meat and potatoes of your business, so you must always be assessing how it is working. The five key areas of your value chain are the blueprint for how to take your value proposition from concept to customer. You must always be assessing whether that engine is running properly. And if there are any problems, the first place you would look is in your value chain.

For example, if customers are getting their t-shirts but it's the wrong order, which part of the value chain do you look in? Outbound logistics would be the place. Something is happening in this part of the value chain that is causing the orders to go to the wrong addresses. Understanding your value chain gives you the ability to troubleshoot these kinds of issues quickly. What if customers are getting their t-shirts, but the design is messed up? What part of the value chain do you look in? Operations is the place to start. Something is going on with the actual printing of the t-shirt. You can go right in and examine what you need to do to clear that up. What if customers are complaining that the quality of the t-shirt itself is bad and could be better? What part of the value chain does this fall into? Inbound Logistics would be the place. We would need to see about getting better quality blank t-shirts to begin with. Everything you need to successfully deliver value to your customer is found in the value chain. This is for any type of business large or small.

Value Chain for Service Businesses

What about if you have service-based businesses? Does the value chain still apply? Yes, it does. Remember that every business has its own unique value chain. You always have stuff coming in and stuff going out to the customer, even if it's information or some type of intellectual property. Inbound logistics could be the different processes you use, or the research you have to do for a client. Operations could be how you arrange the information and ideas into a solution for the client. Maybe you create power point presentations or marketing plans or branding packages. Outbound logistics, of course, is how you deliver the solutions to the client. Remember that not all primary areas of the value chain will be focal points for every business. Service-based businesses are usually very involved with the marketing, sales and services parts of the value chain.

The way you market your service could be the difference maker for your service business. You may have a sales process that works better for potential clients than other businesses in your space. Your after sales engagement could be where you set yourself apart with your service business. The basic understanding is that all the things you do to bring value to your customer is what constitutes the value chain. By breaking down your value chain actions, you can easily see how to get the idea you developed in your value proposition, into the hands of the customers. If you have a service business, you are still trying to deliver an idea into customer hands, it's just not a physical product you are delivering. So the value chain concept remains the same. Remember that all value chains are going to look different. This means that the decisions you make to deliver your services to your customers will be different than your competition. The more efficient you can be with your value chain the cheaper it will be to deliver the service. After the value proposition, the value chain is where you will need to do the most work. Can you utilize technology to deliver your service to your customers at a cheaper cost? Can you use strategic partnerships for things like research?

Examples

Let's walk through a couple more examples to help you with your understanding of the value chain.

Insurance Agency:

Inbound Logistics- What insurance companies are the policies you sell coming from?

Operations- The process for preparing the policy paperwork package for the customers.

Outbound Logistics- How are you getting the policy paperwork package to the customers for signatures, etc.? Is it by mail, or electronically?

Marketing and Sales- How are you getting your customers? How are they hearing about you? Who is out there selling your products?

Service- What if someone has questions about their policy or wants to increase their coverage? (This part of the value chain is probably very important to this type of business. People are always going to have questions after they purchased a policy. No one wants to purchase an insurance policy one day then never be able to speak to the insurance agent after that.)

Bakery:

Inbound Logistics- The process of getting in all your flour, eggs, milk, toppings, spices and other ingredients. Are your ingredients delivered to you daily or maybe weekly?

Operations- Baking the cakes, pies, muffins, donuts, etc., and packaging them up to go out.

Outbound logistics- The pickup or delivery process to the customer after everything is baked and packaged.

Marketing and Sales- How are people hearing about you? How are you making sales? Maybe you have a retail location, or maybe an online store?

Service- What happens if customers have an issue with their order? How would you handle that?

Let's try one more example from a name you know; McDonald's. McDonald's is the king of fast food. Their value chain is engineered to give you a quick and low-cost meal. What areas of their value chain do you think are focal points? Are there any areas that may not be as important? I want you to think about your own experience with this brand. Focus on inbound logistics, operation and outbound logistics. They get all the buns, beef patties, condiments, and potatoes in. They put them together and give them to the customer. They can do all this in minutes because their value chain is engineered for speed. Now let's think about the last two primary areas of the value chain, starting with service. How many times have you gotten home or even a few blocks away from the restaurant and realize they forgot to put cheese on your burger or some other problem? How often do you drive all the way back to get the problem resolved? The answer is not very often. That's because McDonald's is set up to give you quick food at a cheap price. It's not worth it to the average customer to come all the way back to rectify a wrong order. So, they don't spend as much time on the service part of the value chain. There is no extra counter at the local McDonald's that is dedicated to returns or bad orders. Walmart on the other hand, has a whole department dedicated to returns. Service is a big part of their value chain. McDonald's does, however, spend billions and billions of dollars on marketing. You can't turn on the tv or radio (I know, who listens to the radio anymore) without seeing and hearing a McDonald's commercial. They have billboards on the highway as you are driving. They have coupons in your mailbox every week. They sponsor all of your favorite sports events. There are not many companies that spend more money on marketing.

As you can see, it doesn't matter what the business is, the value chain explains the entire process of delivering the value to the customer. **Next to value proposition, the value chain is where all the action is found for any business.** The value proposition gives you an outline of your idea. The value chain brings it to life. Just imagine the number of businesses that try to launch without having a clear understating of value proposition and value chain. They are basically just throwing things against the wall to see what will stick. I have seen many businesses that fall into this category, and it generally ends badly for the entrepreneur. The sad part is that many times the business idea itself was a good one. Entrepreneurs are always seeing opportunities for business. But one of the first things I said in this book is that real success happens when you can take that idea and transition it into an actual business. Understanding value proposition and value chain is the way to make that transition.

CHAPTER 5:

Business Model

What is Your Business Model?

The last piece of the external why that we will discuss is your business model. Now that you have your value proposition and an understanding of the value chain, you should be able to clearly see your business model. The business model is the part of the business that gets the most attention. As you talk to people, especially investors, about your business, the business model is generally the center of attention. Everything we've discussed so far should allow you to clearly see what a good business model for your business would be. So what is a business model? **It's a repeatable and scalable way to exchange value for money.** In short, a business model is how your business makes money, or how you put the cash in the bank. As you can see, this is why everyone would be interested in this part of your business. But you generally can't get to a good business model without following the steps we have laid out so far in the Vision to Value framework.

The business model is a culmination of everything we have discussed so far. Again, it's also the last piece of the external why. The business model puts together the company's products and services, the target customer group, and the company's expenses into a package. These things should sound very familiar to you. All of these things were covered in the first two parts of the external why (the value proposition and the value chain). **Once you put them together, you then identify the way to actually exchange the value this package represents to the customer for their money**.

Repeatable and Scalable

There are two word that must be in place in order for you to have a good business model. You can probably guess what they are by looking at the title of this section: repeatable and scalable. What does this actually mean though? Let's start with repeatable. Remember that a business model is the way by which you exchange value (your product or service) for the customer's money. After hearing the definition again, can you connect the dots? If a business model is the actual way you get money from the customer, it should be a way that you can use a lot of times. That is what repeatable means in the business model world. It means that the way you exchange value for money can be done over and over again. The more time you do it, the more money you can make. This is why the business model is so pivotal. Also why it is the third and final part of the external why.

You all should know me by now. Let's try a quick example to walk through this idea. If you have a great value proposition; meaning that you know your customer, what problem you are solving for them, and what pricing area you want to be in, then you are on the right track. Now let's say you also have worked out a great value chain; meaning you have all the behind the scenes pieces in place to actually do what you laid out in the value proposition. So the first two pieces of the external why are in place and looking great. Now for the business model. Let's say you have to walk 10 miles to engage with each customer, so they can pay you for your service or product. I don't care how in shape you are that is not repeatable. If you had to walk a hundred miles for each customer you would quickly go out of business. This is because you had a great value proposition and value chain, but a horrible business model.

Now let's take that same example and think about scalability. But first, what does having a scaleable business model even mean. It means that you can grow it, or that you can do it anywhere. Using the example above, let's say you are the most athletic and in-shape person in the world, and somehow you are able to walk the 10 miles for each customer. How many people would you be able to hire at your company? It would be difficult to grow (or scale) the business because not many people would apply to work for a company that required a 10 mile walk per customer. This example may be a little farfetched, but it highlights what a business model looks like when it not repeatable or scalable.

What does a scalable and repeatable business model look like then? Facebook would actually be a great example. Facebook makes it free to sign up with them over the internet. First of all it is free. This makes it repeatable. Its easy for anyone to just go on their website and sign up. It is also scaleable because everything is done online. So these free people can easily sign up to Facebook from anywhere around the world; repeatable and scalable.

Can a business model be one without the other? The answer is yes and no. It is possible for your business model to be repeatable but not be scalable. However, it's generally not possible to be scalable without being first repeatable. Going back to our example, let's say you actually find one other person who will walk the 10 miles to see every customer. And the two of you build a successful local business in your neighborhood. We already explained why this business model would not be scalable, but you have found a way to make it repeatable.

Generally business models that successfully engage with people online are repeatable and scalable. The idea behind a good business model is that is allows as many people as possible to **buy your stuff.** Repeatability is often overlooked when entrepreneurs begin selling their product. When an entrepreneur gets a sale, it is very exciting. However, the sale itself should not be the most exciting part of the transaction. The most exciting part, if done right, is the fact that you can use that same process to make 10 sales, 100 sales, and 1,000 sales. That's when you know you have a good business model working. It's wonderful to get one sale, but it's absolutely awesome when you can use that one sale as an example for how you will get 1,000 sales. This is the essence of the business model.

B2B vs B2C

There are many types of business models and many ways to actually sell your products and services to customers. Your job at this point of the external why development process, is figuring out which one works best for your business. To start, you have to determine which category your business fits into. Most businesses fit into two basic categories.

- B2C- Business to Customer. Simply put, your end customers are actual people like me and you.

- B2B- Business to Business. Your customers are not individuals, but other businesses like yours or maybe the hair salon down the street. Imagine that you are a hair spray company and you sell your product to hair salons instead of individual people. That is a B2B business.

There are others, but most businesses will fit into one of these two categories. For example, some businesses sell to governments and some businesses sell to enterprises (large companies like Verizon, Microsoft, Walmart, or Bank of America). This part of the business model should be pretty simple to think about. Remember the first part of your value proposition. Who is you target customer? If you identified a group of people, you have a B2C business. If you identified a set of businesses you want to sell to, it's B2B. We spent an extensive amount of time figuring this out, so you should know right away whether you are selling to people or to businesses, or even to the government. You also understand by now that the value proposition and value chain are going to look different no matter which category your business fits into.

Types of Business Models

Next let's examine the different types of business models. First thing to know is there are many ways to sell your product to your people. Some companies, like car dealerships, have multiple business models. If you go to a dealership, you can pay cash outright for a car, but you can also make monthly payments towards ownership, which is what most people do. If neither of these options work for you, you can also lease a car. Those are three distinct business models all operating at one business. Your business will probably just have one business model, but I use the car dealership to show you it is possible to have more than one. Here a few of the other popular business models you probably see every day but may not have even noticed:

- Leasing Model- Think about car company leases or rental car companies.
- Subscription Model- Think about Netflix, Sling or Hulu.
- Freemium Model- Think about Facebook or Instagram. It's free to join the service. Then they make money from other companies that advertise to all the free people that joined.
- Retail Model- Having a store front that you sell your products or services from.
- Direct to Consumer- You sell to people online with very low overhead cost. Just imagine someone coming to your website and placing an order. You then send that order directly to the person. Or perform your service directly for the person.

These are just a few of the popular ones. I would definitely suggest you Google business models to see the many types that are out there. Do you want to hear something awesome? There are new business models that still have yet to be created. The Freemium Model wasn't really a thing until Facebook came around. They were not the first to use it, but they were the ones to make it popular. They created a business model that is now used all around the world. They now teach whole classes at universities on how disruptive the freemium model has been.

Businesses that do not have a good business model or the right business model will in fact go out of business. But let's not get too complicated. As you all probably know by now, I like to keep it simple and basic. Remember, a good business model tells us how you are going to consistently sell something to a group of people for less than it cost you to produce it. That's all your business model is. And as you see, most of the pieces you need for a good business model you already have from developing the rest of your external why.

Using this logic, what do you think would make the best business models look like? Take a guess. By now you should know that the answer is always going to be whatever works best for your business. The best business models represent the easiest, most efficient, and cost-effective way for your people to buy your stuff. If you are selling $5 costume jewelry, the direct-to-consumer model might be the best way to sell your products. It would be cheaper for you and have a much lower overhead than trying to rent a storefront (retail model). Your customers can easily browse your jewelry, make a selection, and check out online. However, this business model would probably not be the best if you are a barber selling haircuts. The reason is that the barber has to physically be there to cut the customer's hair. The retail storefront model may be the best option. This way people can come to the physical barber shop to get their haircut.

Let's go a little deeper using the barber shop example above. If the barber has a great value proposition and a great value chain but chooses the freemium business model, there may be problems. The freemium business model, just like the direct to consumer model, is traditionally not the best business model for a barber shop business. Here is a side note that I must mention. Always remember that as an entrepreneur you may be able to find creative ways to put any kind of business together with any kind of business model. Just because haircuts are normally sold at barbershops does not mean you can't come up with some crazy new way to sell them with a freemium business model. Always remember that nothing is off limits when building your business. As an entrepreneur and businessman of over 20 years, I had to say that. Vision to Value is a framework to give you the tools and direction to start building. Once you have gone through the framework you may find something new and innovative that you want to try. The main thing is to ensure that the business model matches the value proposition and the value chain, and that all parts of the external why line up.

What is the business model for your business? Remember to keep it simple. Generally, the harder it is to explain your business model the worse it might be. There may be some complexity in the value chain, because that's where all the behind the scene decisions need to be made about how to bring the value proposition to life.

The business model, however, should be very simple to articulate and easy to understand. When people are giving you their money, it should be as smooth a process as possible. The last thing you want is a lot of people wanting your stuff but have a difficult process for them to pay you for it. With all the other steps in place it should become relatively easy to see which business model will work best for you. But make sure it matches up with all the other pieces of the external why.

CHAPTER 6:

The External Wrap Up

The Recap

The external why is as fundamental to your business as breathing is to us humans. You absolutely will not succeed without it firmly in place. Everyone who will ever engage with your company will do so because you have a compelling value proposition, a great value chain and a strong business model. The value proposition outlines your idea, and the value chain gives you the process for bringing it to life. The business model gives you the path to actually complete the sale of your product or service. Everything else you do to further your business builds off of these three things. The external why is the structure that any and every business is built upon. **That's why it is almost pointless to talk about marketing, Facebook ads, and Instagram followers before you nail down your external why.** All the mindset motivation in the world will not get you the business results you are looking for without these key business principles in place. I'll end this section of the book by reiterating that this is the place to start in business. There are experts in branding and marketing, efficiency, mindset, operations, finance, etc. And all these people put out great content with thousands of books and millions of videos. But to successfully bring an idea to the market, you must start with the external why. Everything, and I mean everything, else builds on top. Getting back to the basics is how you build a foundation that will last and increase your likelihood for overall business success. The three areas of the external why are absolutely fundamental.

Now let's discuss the different real-world functions of the external why. I want to highlight a few specific areas.

General Simplicity

The external why itself is not complicated to understand. Any entrepreneur, in any business, of any size, at any point in the business life cycle can understand this framework. The tricky part is bringing the pieces together in a way that works. The way you put the pieces together is what makes your business unique. Every business has the same basic foundation. The successful ones have just managed to put these key areas together better than their competition. That's it. Remember, don't over think it. If you want to be successful, get obsessed with the three areas of your external why. It will really make every other area of your business so much easier to manage.

Keeping it simple is something that took me a long time to learn. I've been involved with all types of business in multiple industries. Once I learned to get back to the basics, no matter what I was looking at, business became so much easier. Once I discovered that there is an actual framework for business success, I immediately began to go to the next level of my business. Another thing I discovered is that super successful businesspeople speak the language of this framework. So keep it simple and let the ideas in this framework lead the thoughts and conversation about your business.

Troubleshooting

Any type of problem with your business can be narrowed down to either your value proposition, your business model or something in the value chain. When I am working with my clients, I can quickly pinpoint the issue they are having because it generally originates in one of these three areas. As we have learned, all three areas have to work in harmony for things to move forward. If there is any misalignment in the external why, there will be an issue. The best businesses are constantly checking to make sure the elements of their external why are functioning properly. Think of the external why like the engine of your car. The car cannot run without the engine. As long as the engine is running smoothly the car can go. Whether the seat gets ripped or the air conditioner stops working, or you get a hole in the floorboard, as long as the engine is working the car will still go. However as soon as the engine goes, you generally have to get rid of the car. The external why is the same way. It is the engine of your business. You want to constantly be checking it, getting oil changes and tune ups so that the business can continue to go forward. If your business has stopped going forward or is slowing down, you must first check the engine.

Starting Up

Just like the troubleshooting example above, if you want to build a new car you start with the engine. For any new idea, start with the external why. I'm going to break this section down into three groups: the entrepreneur, the employee, and the employer. When I think about developing new ideas, these three groups of people come to mind first.

The first group is the entrepreneur, the person that is constantly thinking about ideas. I would know, because that is me. I have been that way since middle school. However, once I began starting businesses, I could not find the blueprint that worked for me. Don't get me wrong, there are businesses geniuses out there who teach business all the time, and I have listened to most of them. I could never find someone who explained the basics in one easy to follow format. There are tons of content on the individual subjects we have discussed in this book. But putting them together in a systemized framework has been empowering. Vision to Value gives entrepreneurs a clear place to start when they have an idea they want to work on. Entrepreneurs can easily follow along as they develop their ideas. Generally, the entrepreneur has to learn by failing. My early business ventures were riddled with mistakes, things that could definitely have been avoided if I had a framework to work from. Having an idea but not knowing where to start is nerve-racking.

The external why is not only a good place for entrepreneurs to start but also for employees at existing companies. This is where a business framework becomes very valuable. Entrepreneurs may not have a framework and a high probability of failure, but they will try an idea anyway. That's just how we are built. Employees who work for organizations have a vastly different approach to innovation and idea creation. An employee may have a great idea for their company but may never act on it, or even mention it, without having a framework to guide them. Innovations from within a company's employee pool are the best because they come from people who are on the frontlines. Generally, they know the inner workings of certain parts of the business better than the CEO. The problem is that those employees will not jeopardize their careers for a new idea like an entrepreneur would. Raise your hand if you are an employee of a company and you know what I'm talking about. The external why is for you! You can take any idea for a new or existing product or service and walk it through the external why. This will give you the information you need to present your idea to management or the board, or even just to see whether it will work or not. The external why will get that idea you have been thinking about for your organization, out of your head and into the real world. And maybe a promotion!

Innovation from Within

Even though we will be discussing the third group, which are employers, I had to formally name this section. If you run an organization, think through the last section from the other side. How valuable would it be to give your employees a tool that increases innovation? People can get intimidated when they are given a blank sheet of paper. By simply lining the paper (giving your employees a framework) to push their ideas through, you will increase the likelihood of getting that innovation from within. There are new ideas floating all through organizations. The tricky part is finding ways to capture them and bring them to the forefront. Different organizations approach this problem in different ways. Some spend a lot of money working to figure this out. The external why is a great place to get your people going. They may not formally know the terms, but employees will probably have a sense of the company's different value propositions, business models and value chains. If they don't, they should. This framework will make it extremely easy to see if, and where a new idea will fit in.

If one of your employees has an idea, you want to make it as easy as possible for it to come out. In the context of your existing business, an employee should be able to say who their idea would be for, what problem it solves, and where they think it would fit on the price spectrum. They should then be able to figure out what the value chain would look like to bring it to customers, and if the idea would need a different business model. This clear and concise thought process will empower your people to at least explore new possibilities.

Unified Communication Framework

The last and most important value the external why brings to the table is a unified language for business communication. A unified communication framework for ideas is something stakeholders on all sides of the table can use (entrepreneurs, employees, employers, investors, board members, executives, managers, etc.). If someone has an idea or wants to vet an idea, this framework provides a place to start. If two people who don't know each other want to connect on a business idea, the external why brings everyone onto the same page. This is powerful because it gives everyone a viable launching point. If the value proposition cannot be clearly articulated, there is much work to do; or maybe no work at all because everyone decides to move on. Either way everyone can sync up on how to start developing an idea because they are speaking the same language.

Rinse and Repeat

Now that we have come to the end of the external why, you should hopefully have 1,000 times more insight about business than you had when you started the book.

The external why breaks down any business or idea very quickly. If you have always had an idea but never knew what to do next, this information will literally save your life. This biggest take away is that you can also now apply this framework for all of your ideas, both present and future. You quite literally can rinse and repeat because this works with every type of business idea. If you are thinking about adding a new product or service, start with the external why. You can take this with you as you grow in business. The external why will save you resources like time and money. You no longer have to blindly try things or not try things for fear of failure. The external why will give you clear direction on what you need to do.

Every idea individually needs to go through this process. Even if you have an existing business and are thinking of expanding into other areas, you must start here. Every product or service you sell is going to need its own set of target customers, and each will bring its own unique value to those customers. Once you get the hang of the Vision to Value framework, you will see the ease of quickly applying it to just about any business situation. If one of your employees come to you with an idea, the first thing you will ask is who it's for and what problem it would solve for them. Although, if you show your employees the Vision to Value framework, they will already have those details together when they show you the idea!

CHAPTER 7:

The Internal Why

What Is the Internal Why?

The second part of this book is dedicated to something that is highly overlooked and under-appreciated when it comes to business. This is especially true with start-ups, early stage companies and small businesses, although I have seen it with larger companies as well. The internal why answers the question of "why" for you and your business. It's the internal reasons why your business is in existence. The internal why tells the story of your business. It's the narrative that radiates from inside the walls of the office. Many businesses spend so much time trying to make money that they never consider the importance of the internal why. Remember this: the external why is what gets people in the doors, but the internal why is why they stay.

So who is impacted by the internal why? The short answer is everybody. So not just your customers, partners and investors, but also you, your employees, your board and your community. A great internal why is the glue that brings all of your stakeholders together. The cohesiveness between those different groups of people is what brings longevity to your business. I know what you're thinking. Can you have a successful business without an internal why? Remember part one of the book, I told you that your business absolutely cannot survive without an external why. Well the internal why is a bit different, in that you can make it without one. The issue is that it will be very difficult to sustain your success over time without a solid internal why.

The external why is the actual foundation that your business stands on, the internal why gives your company a strategic direction. You must know where you want to go. Your employees need to know where you want to go. If not, you will have a group of people working in your company that are all going in their own direction. And that, my friends, will lead to chaos. It may take time, but it's an inevitable result. That why I said you can have a great external why and jump out to a great start, and even make some good success. Eventually however, you will begin to have a mountain of issues popping up in different areas that you can't account for in your external why.

The best way to illustrate the merits of the internal why is to tell you a real story from a real entrepreneur. This is an example from an actual client of mine. I had a client in the real estate business, and they were very successful. They had been in business for 15 years and now they were looking to take their business to the next level. Among other things, they initially talked to me about low morale and high turnover at the company. They even expressed personal anxiety and lack of drive as they personally drove to the office every day. All this was despite doing very well financially. The owner just could not figure out why the business, though doing very well, had plateaued.

Of course, the first thing we discussed together was the external why (because that's always where you start). The owner could easily and adequately explain the value proposition, the value chain and the business model. The external why was locked in! They had built a very successful real estate business predominantly in the REO space. For those that don't know, REO stands for Real Estate Owned. It's basically properties that don't sell in foreclosure auctions because the original owner defaulted on the loan. REO is generally about real estate transactions that are available, in large part, because of people who are in bad situations.

At this point we realized that the owner had a well-oiled machine that they could articulate and write a book on. I then turned to the internal why. When my client had a good and compelling external why, I was pretty sure we would find their issue by examining the internal why. Once I began asking about the mission, the purpose and overall vision of the business, the successful and wealthy business owner looked like a deer caught in the proverbial headlights. They said they had never thought about it in all their 15 years of business. They said they didn't even know to think about it.

So I asked them to, just off the top of their head, tell me what they want the company to be known for and stand for. Just as quickly and succinctly as they gave the external why, they gave me the vision of the company that was important to them. Some of the main things my client mentioned were: empowering people through real estate. Also, helping people build wealth and generational wealth, while educating underserved communities on the power of real-estate investing. The owner spoke effortlessly about basically wanting to serve people in multiple ways through real estate. I immediately saw what the issue was. The external why and the internal why were conflicting with one another. The owner wants the company to help the community, but most of the company's money was made from people who were basically getting kicked out of their properties. That's why morale was low at the company, and why my client felt anxiety about going to work every day. That's also why turnover was high. Who would want to work for a company that the owner doesn't want to work for? Needless to say, the owner was blown away that we were able to get down to root causes so quickly. We were then able to discuss how to turn things around and develop a plan to take the business to the next level. My client ended up exiting the REO space all together. They transitioned into areas of real estate that were more closely aligned with the vision of the company. Happy to say that the business is doing extremely well today.

Were you able to see how the internal why and the external why did not line up with one another? Were you able to see the issues that it presented? My client had literally grown to dislike the very thing that was giving them success. All because they did not have a vision.

The internal why gives your business a sense of purpose and gives your people a reason to believe. You must be able to align your external and your internal why to truly have sustainable business success. You can't get off the ground without a compelling external why, but you can't stay off the ground without a compelling internal why. Like my client, you can have the best external why, but you will eventually hit a roadblock without a firm understanding of why you get up in the morning and devote your time to the company. The employees need to know the same. Just like a seed needs to be planted in soil much larger than itself to grow, a business needs to be planted in a vision much larger than itself to grow. If not, your business will constantly hit a wall. Or even worse, your business will grow with no direction and self-destruct.

What are the steps for developing your internal why? Even though these steps will be based heavily on personal convictions, the overall formula is very concrete (as you see from my client's situation). Just by going through these steps my client was quickly able to turn it around. The internal why is not a sideshow that you come back to. The first thing to know is that the internal why is a solid building block on the road to success. It's just as important as any of the other business components we have discussed. However, we are not going to hold hands and hope that some magical purpose descends upon us. Some people think the internal why is a mystical, pie-in-the-sky thing that doesn't really add value. But nothing could be further from the truth. The internal why is about using your personal convictions to set concrete boundaries for your business to follow. Your personal convictions are just that, your convictions. The business will harness that energy to gain a strategic focus for the future.

There are many ways that people teach the internal why. Because I like simplicity, I break "internal why" down into just two categories: Vision and Mission. These two things will be one of your business's unique identifiers in the market because they will drive the choices you make in all areas of your business. Since everyone has different personal convictions, businesses that are even in the same industry will make fundamentally different decisions. The vision and mission will not only guide the decisions you do make, but also the decisions you don't make, which can be even more important.

The Narrative

Now that you have a clear understanding of what the internal why is, I need to spend a few minutes really highlighting why it is so important. We have had some great discussion about the internal why up to this point, but the narrative is where it all comes together. Your internal why shapes the overall narrative behind your entire company, the big idea. You as the entrepreneur must be able to tell your story. The general purpose of the internal why is to help you to do just that.

I have seen brilliant entrepreneurs who've had some great ideas but did not know how to tell their story. Telling your story and conveying your message is just as important as the product itself. It may be even more important. The narrative is what people connect to. It's the thing that keeps them invested in your business's success. When I say invested, I'm not just talking about money. I'm talking about a customer who will tell others about your business, share, post and like on social media because of the way your company makes them feel. This is what a good narrative does for your business. How are you telling your story?

Once you have gone through the steps laid out for your external why, you must be able to touch people mentally and emotionally. The best way to start this process is by writing down a vision and mission. Answer all the questions we discussed in the previous chapters. This will help you think through all the reasons for why you do what you do. The vision and mission are generally short statements that anyone can read to get an understanding of what you stand for. For you as the entrepreneur however, these statements are just the beginning of a story only you can tell to connect people to your business. Now before you tell me you are not a storyteller, I urge you to try it. If you absolutely can't tell the story yourself it may be good to bring someone in who can. Maybe hire a coach who can help you take your internal why and expand it into the narrative that drives the company. I have done it for many clients.

Let's think about some real-world examples that explain the importance of the story behind the actions a business makes. Think about the local high school in your area. Every year in the spring, the high school seniors do car washes to help raise money for the class senior trip. They set up in the parking lot of the local Walmart and put out signs and banners and play lots of cool music. A few people stand out in the street trying to get people to turn in and get their car washed. You may have driven by 10 gas station car washes since you left your house that day. Some of those gas stations even say you can get a few cents off your gas if you buy a car wash, but you continue to drive by anyway. However, when you see that these seniors want to wash your car so they can raise money for their senior trip, you turn in and get a car wash. Why does this happen? It is because you connected to the story behind the car wash.

Ok here is another one. I heard Simon Sinek, who I mentioned earlier, use this example. Let's say there is a young girl in your neighborhood who is selling glasses of lemonade at her lemonade stand on a hot summer day. She is selling those cups of lemonade for $3 each so she can save money to buy a new bike. Of course, you could go to the store and buy a whole two liter for half that price. But you buy five glasses for you and your whole family because of the story behind the cup of lemonade. How about Chick-fil-A, arguably the home of the best fast food chicken sandwich. Chick-fil-A is closed on Sundays. One of the core values of their internal why is the belief in people and family. They believe that one day a week should be devoted to spending time with loved ones. This is a story they tell in everything they do, from their commercials, to interviews, to online advertisements. They close their stores one day a week to allow their employees to spend time with families. This just makes you appreciate their over-the-top customer service even more. What a great story!

Remember, the narrative around your business is the essence of your internal why. Your vision and mission, which we will discuss next, are a great place to start but think deeper about how you would actually tell someone why you started your business. The vision and mission are abbreviated statement for a story you must be able to tell. You have to be able to connect. Think about the excitement in that high school senior's eyes as they tell you about the exotic place their class is going to go if they can just raise enough money. Or the glimmer in that little girl's eye when she tells you she almost has enough to buy the new bike. When you find out that she is close to getting her new bike, maybe you call a few of your neighbors so they can come out and buy some lemonade too. The story is what can drive people to action. Since your story is unique, it will be different from the story that all of your competitors are telling for their companies. If your story (internal why) is more compelling than your competitors, your business will be the choice for the customer. That means your story can literally give you a competitive advantage.

I'm not saying you have to tell people a sob story. I'm simply saying your internal why should reflect what you believe. It only needs to be authentic to be real. Imagine the fit health coach who has had to battle back from obesity to start their health coaching business. After that person has developed the external why for their health coaching business (to make sure the business idea makes sense), they can develop an internal why that tells the story of how their experience makes them passionate to help others. Don't ever be afraid to tell your story. It is yours, and it is what makes you unique.

Let's say there are two IT security companies that are competing for the same customer. Company A and B both are about the same on the external why, meaning that the businesses are similar in their function. In this scenario, the internal why is what might determine who gets the customer. Let's say company A does not have an internal why. But company B does have one. Company A may talk about their technology and their prices during their presentation. Company B will do the same thing but also talk about vision to keep the world's digital information safe. Company B will also talk about how the CEO started the company after his personal identity was stolen, and he did not want to see that happen to anyone else. This is a hypothetical scenario, but which company do you think would win the customer? I would suggest it is company B, because of the narrative. The story they were able to tell about why they do what they do is what will ultimately help to capture the client.

Vision

The vision is an overall long-term outlook of where you want your company to be. Think 20, 30, or even 40 years down the line. Think about how you would be talking about your company at your retirement party as you look back. I know you may be thinking, is this necessary? You're just a start-up or very young company and you just want to keep the lights on today. I guarantee you the time you spend on your internal why will be worth its weight in gold as you grow. The vision is an overarching idea that makes you want to get up every day and dedicate your life and time to this business. I always tell my students the bigger the better. If your vision is something that can be accomplished in a year, it is too small. That would be something more like a goal. A vision should be something your kids are still trying to achieve with the business after you leave it to them. I know this type of big thinking makes some people nervous, but don't overthink it. Like I said in the beginning, this doesn't have to be some sort of deep thing. You just need to give your business a bit of a guiding light to lead you down the path.

Vision is something that I'm going to help you draw out in this part of our discussion. I say draw out because that is exactly what we will be doing. The vision isn't something you should have to create. It should already be somewhere inside of you. You may not necessarily be able to articulate it at this moment, but it's in there. I'm simply going to help you put words to something that you are already carrying within. So as we draw out your vision, remember that you are totally in control of how this portion of the internal why turns out.

Your vision can also evolve over time as you get older, or more fortified in your convictions. Or maybe you're like my client who hadn't created a vision for 15 years and just hit a wall. Either way the vision can grow with you, but you must start today with something. One suggestion I can make is to think about stakeholders. Stakeholders are all the people who are impacted by the business you do. Maybe you take your stakeholders into account when writing your vision. Thinking about those who are touched by your business is a sure way to begin considering a long-term vision. What do you want your company to be known for? What do you want customers to see when they peel back the layers of the company? What about employees? When they decide to come and work for your company, what do they get there?

Another thing to know when writing down your vision is that it has to be true to you. It's better to just be honest about the things that are important to you. I know someone out there is saying this all sounds a little pie-in-the-sky and just wants to make money. Well guess what, it's ok to say that too. The key is that you have something that guides you. If you just want to make money, that can certainly be your vision. At least people will know up front that this is what's most important to the company.

The powerful thing about the internal why is that it can be whatever you want it to be. Your vision can be to make the most money in your industry. That's a big vision that you can plant your business into, and guess what, it will grow. You will attract people who only want to make money. People who are all about the money will love it at your company. You may run into an issue with people potentially doing "anything" to get the money, which could definitely be harmful down the line. The main point here is that your vision sets the tone for how your business does what it does.

Crafting your vision is by no means an exact science. Again, you need to have something that guides your business into the future. If you don't set a vision the business will take off in its own direction and everything will sound like a good idea for the business. Think of vision as the lens by which you filter all of your decisions. It's just like putting on a pair of sunglasses. If you have a vision, all your decisions will be influenced by the thought of where you ultimately want to end up. This kind of thought process will keep you on a specific path.

The process of using vision to guide decisions is very much in line with everything we have discussed up to this point. It's all about having a formula in place that helps you make decisions. It makes your business life very simple. If your vision is to give back to the community, you would not partner with a company that is known for taking from the community, no matter how much money the deal presents. That's an easy decision. Here is where it gets interesting. If you do not have a vision, the potential money from the deal may sound good. **The decision is not as easy when there is no guiding thought.** When you have a vision, you don't need to meet with the board, and you don't need to sleep on it. The things that are not pushing you towards your vision become overwhelmingly clear.

Somebody reading this may be saying, well I just have a carwash or a beauty salon, or a cleaning service. I don't need a vision for these types of businesses. That sounds good for the big companies but not for me. My advice to you would be to simply give it a try. Having a guiding thought, even with small businesses, makes a huge difference. Take some time to write out a vision and use it over the next few months as the guiding thought for your business. I guarantee, you will see a major change in how you make business decisions.

Let's say you do have a carwash business and your vision is to have a chain of affordable carwash services all throughout your state. If someone says to you, "this is a great car wash, you should double your prices", you easily know that's not a good idea because your vision is to have a chain of "affordable" car washes. All you would do is thank them for the compliment and keep on moving. Now let's take the same scenario and assume the business owner does not have a vision. He may take that customer feedback and decide he should double his prices. It sounds good because the customer said it and the business could make more money. Not having something to guide your decisions will allow the business to take off in its own direction. It would be like a wild bull running recklessly through town. It almost always ends in disaster. Having a vision is a concrete and effective tool for any business of any size.

One important question I get from early stage companies is: how do you focus on the long-term vision while trying to keep the doors of the business open today? If you were thinking this, it's a great question. The vision is something that you set simply to give you a direction. As many successful entrepreneurs know, the path to actually getting to success will be this zigzag, winding path that seems to be all over the place. The key is that while you are traveling on this crazy path, you have a target that you can constantly be looking at. Once you set the vision, it doesn't overwhelm your everyday thinking. It rather acts as a guide you can keep with you as you're out there kicking butt and taking names day in and day out.

So, how do write a vision? I'm glad you asked. Below we will track through a few questions you can consider when writing your vision. These questions will make you look ahead. Remember the vision is already in you. This process is all about bringing it out. Take a few minutes to consider where you will be down the line. If some of the questions start to feel a bit redundant, it's ok. I just want you to think about your vision from different perspectives. Lastly, give yourself permission to dream and think ahead. Even if it is uncomfortable, step out of your box for a few moments to consider the following questions.

What is it about you and your business that people value?

This question really gets at the heart of what will ultimately make your business successful, and that is YOU! It all starts with you. The way you view things and the way you approach the business will be infused into all areas of the company. As you think ahead, how do you want people to view you? Will they say that you were a visionary? Will they say that you cared about people and worked hard to make a difference? What will people say when your name comes up at the water cooler? Will people be happy to work with and for you? Think through these things and write down how you want to be considered.

What has your business achieved?

Remember, it's ok to dream. Is your company a million-dollar company? Billion-dollar company? Trillion-dollar company? I know there is someone out there that cringed when they read the words billion and trillion. So often people automatically assume that they can't do a certain thing. They will say, billion, well that's not for me. There is no way I can make a billion dollars. My response to you is that you can. Just for a moment, allow yourself to say crazy things. Write down things that resonate with you. What are the things that you are proud of about your business? What would make you look back at your business and feel like you have accomplished something? Is there one specific part of your business that gives you fulfillment? As you start to give your responses, you should start to see the things that are ultimately important to you. If you want these things to be important years down the line, you should prioritize them in your vision today.

What difference has your business made in people's lives?

Let's look outwardly at the people you serve. Think specifically about the value you want to add to your people. What will they say about you? After you answer that question, think a bit bigger. Have you been able to add value to the community that your business is in? Will the community be able to say the they are better off because your business has been working in that community?

What shows you that your business has been a success?

How do you ultimately judge whether you have been successful? It's different for different people. Maybe money is not the ultimate thing for you. Maybe it's people, community, family, or legacy. Maybe it's a combination of many different things. Whatever it may be, you can decide what different components of success mean to you. The things that are most important to you should be at the center of this question. The things that drives you today will be reflected in how the business is shaped in the future. How has your business helped you to achieve your goals and dreams? Has the business shaped you in certain ways?

What can you see around you?

This will require you to use your imagination just a little bit more. Close your eyes and imagine 20 years down the line. Now, with your eyes closed, look around and notice what you see. Do you see family around you? Are you in your big mansion? Do you hear the ocean outside of your beachfront condo? Go for a second to that place, then write down what you see.

All of the above questions are meant to make you think of things in a future tense. You can arrange the questions however you want or ask different questions all together. The key is that you project yourself forward to capture what you and the business look like in that frame. This is beneficial because the things that will come to the forefront or the important things. When thinking ahead that far, you are forced to really consider the things that ultimately matter to you. Generally, when people think they will spend the next 25 years on a project, bigger expectations start coming out. This is the essence of what your vision should be. Again, it's not an exact science that works the same way for every business and entrepreneur. As noted in the questions, everyone has different convictions and different things that inspire them. By tapping into this inspiration, you can set the tone for every stakeholder that engages with your company. All business successes and failures start at the top. This means that your business outcome rests squarely on your shoulders. Everything in your business will flow from the top down. Once you tap into your internal reservoir of inspiration to set a vision, it will permeate throughout all parts of the business because it's coming from YOU! Your vision is the first part of the internal why because it's the barometer by which your business will be measured.

Key Takeaways

Your vision is the larger shaping tool for your entire business. It is the first part of your "Internal Why." It is very broad but gives a snapshot of the overall impact you want to have. Your vision begins to tell your story. It gives people an insight of what your values are, and what is important to you. Most importantly, your vision MUST be bigger than you. The bigger the better when it comes to your vision. Your vision should constantly be giving your business something to reach for. When you have something larger that you are striving for its easier to inspire your customers and all the other people who are around you.

Mission

The mission represents the actions you do daily to achieve the overall vision. The mission is much more present and action oriented. When I think of mission, I think of the military going on a mission. It's the set of short-term actions the troop has to take to achieve an overall goal or vision. So what actions are you and your employees doing daily to achieve the vision you came up with in the previous chapter? Again, this does not have to be perfect. But you, as a business owner, must have something to use as your daily north star, to guide each small decision, every day in every department. The vision and the mission generally work in tandem. The vision is the big goal, and the mission outlines the main few things you do daily to get there.

One of the easiest ways to understand mission is to just look at a few companies that we have all heard of. There are plenty of companies out there that have some great mission statements. I would encourage you to look up some of your favorite companies to see what their mission statements are. Since the mission is public, it's generally found right on the homepage of the website. Google your favorite company and it's probably right there. When you do look up your favorite company's mission, I want you to see if it personally connects to you. Chances are that you like the company because of what they stand for. Whether you have ever thought about it before, their mission resonates with you on some level. Here are a couple of good ones we can talk about.

- Tesla (one of my favorite companies)- "To accelerate the world's transition to sustainable energy."
- TED- "Spread ideas."
- LinkedIn- "To connect the world's professionals to make them more productive and successful."
- PayPal- "To build the web's most convenient, secure, cost effective payment solution."
- Amazon- "To be the earth's most customer-centric company, where customers can find and discover anything they might want to buy online, and endeavors to offer its customers the lowest possible price."

- Nordstrom- "To give customers the most compelling shopping experience possible."

As you can see, a mission statement can be short and sweet or long and descriptive. In either case, they are effective. Notice they all have action words in them. The vision doesn't necessarily have to have action in it because it's more of a destination. The mission tells everyone what you do on a day in and day out basis. The mission acts as a guide for the decisions each employee will make daily. The mission explains very concisely why employees get up out of bed and come to their job. If you work at LinkedIn, everything you do daily should be to connect the world's professionals and make them more productive and successful. No matter the department or job description at the company, this mission will guide your actions.

You can see how the vision differs from the mission. The vision is more long term and gives the overall direction. It's there to give you a general sense of direction; a compass for where you are going. The mission is much more tactical and action oriented. The mission is also much more in view of the public. As I said, the mission of most companies is generally found on the front page of the website. This is to signal to the reader that this is what we are doing right now to move ourselves forward as an organization. It brings unity for the employees, and clarity for the customer. If you are a professional and you called LinkedIn's headquarters right now, you can be assured that whoever picks up the phone is trying to connect you and make you more productive and successful. That's the mission of the company. This is the action at the core of their internal why. If you called them for any other reason, they would quickly, and hopefully politely, end the call, because they don't have time to do anything else.

Elon Musk gave us one of the best examples of how a mission can guide daily decisions. In case you don't know, Elon Musk is the second richest person in the world (as I'm writing this book today). Elon gave a talk to the United State Air Force in 2019. It was an excellent interview, and definitely one I would recommend you check out on Youtube. During this interview he was asked about his company Tesla. Tesla is currently (as I'm writing this book) the most valuable car company in the world. Tesla specializes in electric cars and sustainable energy. The Air Force General that was interviewing him asked why Elon Musk did not protect Tesla's technology with patents. Elon Musk replied that keeping his technology away from the world would not be consistent with Tesla's mission. From above, Tesla's mission is "To accelerate the world's transition to sustainable energy." Elon said that the fastest way for the world to transition to sustainable energy is for many companies around the world to do what his company is doing. He added that Tesla cannot do it alone. Tesla has spent billions of dollars developing their technology. They then make their technology available to any company that wants to use it, simply because of their mission. I'm sure at some point the legal department came to Elon and said, "should we start filing the patents for all of the company's technology?" For Elon the answer was a simple no, because filing patents to keep the technology a secret would go against the company's mission.

The mission needs to be at the forefront of everything you do. Some companies put the mission at the bottom of all emails, or on the wall as soon as you walk into the office. I've seen pins and posters, coffee mugs and banners on websites. Companies put the mission everywhere they can squeeze it in because it tells employees, customers and every other stakeholder what they do every day to bring value.

I was on LinkedIn one day scrolling. I'll admit I got caught in the social media trap where you find yourself scrolling for 10 minutes before you even realize it. Anyway, I came across a woman who posted a very relevant message for our discussion. I'm paraphrasing, but essentially she stated in bold letters that LinkedIn is NOT a dating site. She went on to mention the mission of LinkedIn itself. She went on a bit more, admonishing someone in particular (I'm guessing). The key is that even your customers believe what you say your mission is. They even expect other customers who engage with your business to also understand the mission.

Here are some questions you can consider when writing a mission. As you will recognize, these questions begin to overlap from the other topics we have discussed in this book. The redundant nature of this thought process is meant to reinforce the feeling and ideas you have developed up to this point. As you are answering these questions, use the concept of "mission" to guide your thought process. I want you to think about action as you answer. Think about the things you do or will be doing on a regular basis. The high-end clothing store Nordstrom does everything in their power "to give customers the most compelling shopping experience possible". That's their mission, that's it. Doesn't matter whether you are a cashier, a merchandiser, or a salesperson, this is your goal every single day. If someone wants a glass of Champagne while they purchase a $10,000 suit, Nordstrom makes it happen.

Why are you in this business?

Remember that everything you do in business comes down to answering the question "why?" I know it still may sound too simple to be true but it's the secret sauce of any successful business. The successful companies just answer the question of "why" for multiple different groups of people simultaneously. That juggling act is truly where the money is. So why are you in business? Why do you do what you do? Identifying this answer will give you a foundation for some actions you may want to take. As we have walked through the internal why, you may have already answered this question. If that is the case, look at your answer and see what action you can pull out. For example, if you are doing your business to make your community a better place, maybe you can think about the action of service. How does your business serve your community?

How do you treat or want to treat your customers and employees?

This question is the other side of the coin. The first question was meant for you to consider how YOU fit into the business. This question considers two of your main stakeholder groups: your customers and your employees. Again, you may have already given this some thought. Now is the time to pen a few words that bring those thoughts to life. Think of words that reflect your feelings towards your stakeholders. As I always say, don't overthink it. Whatever words resonate, focus in on them and think how they would affect your stakeholders. Once you think of how you would treat customers and employees, think of the actions you need to take to consistently make them feel this way. What comes out should be aligned with how you answered the first question. How you feel about the business and how you feel about your stakeholders should be the same.

What's your big idea?

Next let's talk about the secret sauce a bit. This question should be very easy to manage because of the work you did on value proposition. So what's the hook? What's the important piece that makes your business unique? We talked about LinkedIn earlier. In the increasingly crowded space of social media, they saw an opportunity to create a platform that only focused on business professionals. That was their big idea. They put the word "professionals" right in the mission statement. You can use the same process for your business. Is there a main thing that you can point to that really gets at the heart of what you do? Remember the third part of your value proposition. You may be saying that you want to be the low-cost provider of your industry, which means there isn't anything unique. Well your low-cost strategy is your secret sauce. So maybe your mission has to do with providing your community or your people a low-cost option of something served to them with dignity and respect. It can sometimes be good to include elements of your main thing in your mission. It can give people a clear understanding of what you are consistently doing to stay engaged with them while pushing the company forward.

These are just a few sample questions you can use to begin thinking through your mission. They are here to help you think about the key things that you need to always be doing. If you already work for a company, there should already be a mission by which the company operates; and you should know it by heart. If you don't know it, take some time to learn it. You must know the values of the company that you work for. You have to know the company's internal why. Everything you do for the company should line up with the mission of the company. If you are in accounting at a company, and your boss asks you to lie about the numbers on the quarterly report, while the mission talks about trust and integrity; you know there is a big problem.

Now that you have a good vision and a good mission, we can start to complete the picture of your business. We started with a blank sheet of paper. We outlined your business with the external why and now we've colored it in with the convictions of your internal why. If you have been able to follow along you should have a very strong path forward. The internal and external why are probably the most potent combination of business artillery available to all business owners and entrepreneurs.

I have talked about vision and mission for the internal why. You may want to layer your internal why with other things. Some companies like to use things like purpose statements and statements of values. The main thing to know is that your business must stand for something. This will help guide just about every decision you make. If all decisions made at the company are filtered through the lens of your internal why, you will have unbelievable consistency with those who engage internally and externally with your business.

CHAPTER 8:

Alignment

What is Alignment?

Alignment is the key to longevity. Sustainable business depends on how well the internal and external parts of your business line up with one another. So far, we have taken a step by step journey on how to build each part of your external and internal why. Inevitably we have touched on alignment throughout our discussion. Now we will hit the topic head on, because it will make all the difference for you. Your external and internal why must be aligned. In other words, what you do outwardly has to be in sync with what you say inwardly. Major companies have run into substantial problems when the two were misaligned. Someone said a great statement to me one time. They said it is ok to throw a rock concert, it is also ok to throw a jazz concert, but it's not ok to throw a rock concert and advertise it as a jazz concert.

Alignment is being consistent with all of your stakeholders all of the time. The concept of alignment will drive much of your approach to making decisions. Too often businesses make decisions based solely on certain financial implications, basically how much money will be made. Again, there is nothing wrong with that, but don't advertise your business as one that cares about community or the environment. As I am writing this book in 2020, there is more emphasis on stakeholder engagement than ever before. It is almost impossible to be all about the money and still be successful in today's business environment.

There is an unprecedented focus today on things like climate change, diversity and inclusion, and equality. People want to be connected to companies that are having a positive impact on all of their stakeholders, to include the environment and the planet. You can have the best products with the best value proposition, but if your products are made with child slave labor, it would not matter. People feel like the companies they patronize should want to have a positive impact. Even if you don't have some huge earth saving vision and mission, it's ok. You just want to make sure you are staying true to what you do stand for. Your mission could be about simply providing excellent customer service. If that's the case, you would want to hire employees who are great at customer service. You would want to give great customer service to your customers. If someone engaged with your business and received bad customer service, it would be misaligned with your mission. You wouldn't accept investment dollars from investors who are not concerned with customer service either.

These are all major decisions business owners have to make every day. A strong internal why makes all of these decisions much more streamlined. The fast food chain Chik-fil-a has made customer service a core part of their internal why. You can tell that engaging the customers with a personal touch is something that is very important to the company. It would probably be difficult to get a job at Chik-fil-a if you don't like people and are not a very friendly person yourself, because hiring that person would go against something that is core to Chik-fil-a's internal why. They make sure that there is alignment between their internal and the external why. If you have made it this far in the book, the idea of alignment should be very easy to understand.

The Real World

Now let's bring this conversation into the real world. How does having an internal why truly look on the day to day level? We will now walk through a few examples. Some are hypothetical, and some are brands you know and love. As we are working through these examples, I want you to put yourself in the place of the customer and other stakeholders. Don't just view this from the lens of an entrepreneur or business owner. Think holistically about the different points of view. This will allow you to personalize these principles as you apply them to your business and ideas.

Imagine you own a vegan food company whose vision is to bring healthy, vegan food options to minority and underserved communities. Let's also say you have worked through the external why and the business is now operating smoothly. Here are some scenarios to test your understanding of your internal why.

Scenario 1: What if there is a pork producer and processor that offers you $100,000 for a partnership. They want to build a plant in the minority community you serve and need a better image to get it done. What would you do? The correct answer should be an easy no. This partnership should not even take you very long to consider. Think about your internal why, which is to bring vegan food options to minority and underserved community. After you consider the internal why, this is not the right partnership for multiple reason. What reason can you see? The one that jumps out at me right away is that this is a pork company and you are a vegan company. That already makes this a non-starter because it is not consistent with your internal why. What else jumps out at you?

Scenario 2: Let's say your business has done pretty well and now you need to hire an additional employee. You have done interviews and it comes down to two candidates. Both seem like they would be a good fit. During the interviews you discover that one candidate is a practicing vegan and the other eats meat. Or maybe of the two candidates, one lives in the neighborhood you are serving and the other has to drive twenty miles to get there. In both cases the choice become obvious when you use your internal why to make the decision. The candidate the lives in the neighborhood and is a vegan aligns more with your internal why.

I hope you are beginning to see the power of having an internal why. It doesn't have to be anything super deep. It just needs to reflect what you think is important and what the business stands for. Entrepreneurs have to make hundreds of decisions a month concerning their businesses. The internal why becomes an advantage you will have to navigate the industry you are trying to participate in. Competition is tough, and staying in the game requires businesses to be almost surgical with the moves they make. Precise actions will fuel your success. I'm not saying you won't make mistakes, because you will. What I am saying is that you have to always be moving in a certain direction, even in your failures. The internal why will be that guide.

Here is another one. Walmart is a company that just about everyone has heard of. Walmart is one of the most successful low-cost stores in the world. It is hard to find the things you need cheaper than you can find them at Walmart stores. Their external why is pretty easy to see. If you have ever been to a Walmart, you can easily see their value proposition at work. They are a one-stop-shop with everything you need at the cheapest prices. However, about 15 years ago Walmart was facing a major public relations crisis. But before we examine the crisis, here is Walmart's vision statement, mission statement and core values (all of which you can simply google to learn more about). You have to see their internal why to understand the crisis.

Vision Statement: "Be the destination for customers to save money, no matter how they want to shop."

Mission Statement: "To save people money so they can live better"

Core Values: Service to the customer, Respect for the individual, Strive for excellence, and Act with integrity.

As you read these statements, you can begin to see the internal why of Walmart. They want to focus on people and helping them to live better lives. However, about 15 years ago Walmart was not looked at favorably. People certainly did not think they were helping people. They were hated by all of the new towns and cities they wanted to enter. Walmart was viewed as a small business killer. They were accused of not paying their workers good wages or offering adequate benefits. They also were involved in a bribery case. These are all things you can Google to learn more about. Walmart is a very interesting case study. You should definitely read more about it when you get a chance. There was a period of time when Walmart made a number of missteps that caused a severe loss of public trust. Now remember the statements above. You get a good warm and fuzzy feeling when you think of Walmart's internal why. The problem they were having is that some of their choices did not line up with their internal why. It's as simple as that. They were accused of unethical and questionable things when "Act with Integrity" is written in their core values statement.

If you use the internal why as a guiding light, the right choices Walmart should have made, become pretty clear. Also let me point out the example I made earlier in the book. I gave a personal client example of a business that had a great external why, but was struggling because they did not have the guidance of an internal why. Similar to my client's example, Walmart has the external why down to a science. Even though people may not always like Walmart, they have the lowest price and best product selection. They are so dialed in to their external why that they can make $500 billion in one year. The alignment of the internal why is where their issues began to occur. Over the past decade or so, Walmart has taken significant steps to get their actions back aligned with their internal why. The result is that they are no longer viewed the way they were 20 years ago. Their public image has drastically improved.

The Wrap Up

As you can see, it does not matter the size of the business. Walmart is a $500 billion company, but we can easily walk through their issues using the Vision to Value framework. Vision to value is an easy-to-understand way to quickly asses or develop your business or ideas. It is also the absolute starting place when developing an idea or building a business from scratch. For those that work at a company, knowing the Vision to Value framework will allow you to see insights about your company that others may not see. Instead of employees simply working at a company for a salary, they can now have a quick and easy framework to understand the company's core business, core values and how they line up together. I believe every employee, owner, entrepreneur and leader should have this basic knowledge of the company they are a part of. It helps centralize the entire organization around the main ideas that matter.

CHAPTER 9:

Examples from the Brands We Love

Tesla

Tesla is one of my absolute favorite companies. I mentioned them earlier in the book, but I wanted to dive a little deeper. For those that may not be familiar, Tesla is owned by Elon Musk. This company has single-handedly changed the world by bringing sexy, high performance electric cars to the market. Our world has operated on nonrenewable energy like oil and coal for years and years. No matter how you feel about it, the science says that humans are causing all kinds of damage to the planet like climate change because of this. Tesla has made the entire world begin to shift to sustainable and renewable energy. They have done this with products like their cars, their solar panels, and their battery storage devices. Tesla is one of the most valuable companies in the world and Elon Musk is one of the richest people in the world (as I write this book). And because Tesla has been so successful, other car companies and energy companies are now scrambling to try to keep up.

So how would you break down this company? Remember if you want to understand a company, no matter the size, start with the Vision to Value framework. Understanding the why for all of Tesla stakeholders is how you get to the core of the company. Vision to Value breaks down into two parts, the external why and the internal why (I know this is all review for you at this point). Tesla makes a lot of products. For the sake of this discussion we are only going to focus on their car business. Let's quickly examine the main questions found in the Vision to Value framework:

Who are their customers?

What problem are they solving?

Where are their products on the price spectrum?

What does the value chain look like for Tesla?

What is their business model?

What is Tesla's mission?

Tesla is interesting because they have multiple target customer groups. They sell different cars targeted at different people at different price points. Like most car companies, different models are priced to attract different groups of people. Tesla is the same. Their most expensive car is around $200,000. Their least expensive car is around $35,000, and they are planning to release a car soon for $25,000 to attract even more people to their brand. They have a range of target customers with cars for each category of people.

Remember that all the pieces of the external why have to match up. Tesla would not be trying to sell a $200,000 car to the person looking for a $35,000 car. When Tesla first started 20 years ago, they only sold the expensive $200,000 car. In order for them to eventually bring in the $35,000 buyer, they had to start producing a $35,000 car. This may sound obvious, but it was a lot harder for them to accomplish this than you might think. They had to totally reevaluate their value chain to be able to make a $35,000 car. Think back to chapter four of the book, the value chain is what brings the value proposition to life. The value chain represents all that goes in to make your product or service come out the other end. As I just mentioned, their initial value proposition was to make an expensive, $200,000, clean energy electric car for high end buyers. Their value chain was set up to make that happen. The moment Tesla decided to make a $35,000 for a lower end buyer they had to change their entire value chain. For instance, they had to find a way to get everything cheaper, like raw materials, labor, parts, etc. in order to sell a cheaper car.

Now think about your business. Every time you want to launch a new product or service what are the steps? You must first validate the idea by working out the value proposition. Then you immediately have to work on your value chain to bring it to life. Tesla may be a billion-dollar business, but they had to do the same exact thing. They decided on a new product for people who can't afford to spend $200,000. They then had to create a value chain to match that decision.

One more interesting thing about Tesla's value chain is that they don't spend money on marketing. Remember, not every business will have a focus on every area of the value chain. They completely bypass the marketing and sales part of the value chain. I know you are asking: how do people find out about their cars then? The answer is by word of mouth. They have never spent a cent on marketing since they started the company 20 years ago. They found it better for their business to not spend money on the marketing part of the value chain. Other car companies spend billions of dollars on the marketing and sales part of the value chain. When Tesla decided to sell a cheaper car, they had to find cheaper ways to work their value chain. They have been able to cut billions of dollars from their value chain by simply not spending money on marketing and sales.

Now let's discuss Tesla's business model. Their business model is an online direct to consumer model. Tesla doesn't have stores. Customers come to the website, pick their car, and Tesla delivers it to their house. Tesla's business model looks like one you would see for a local t-shirt business. We discussed that example earlier.

Customers can simply use a website to manage their entire relationship with a company from sales to service. This comparison should show you how universal these business principles are. The same business model that works for a small t-shirt start up, can also work for a billion-dollar car company. If your company uses a direct to consumer business model, you are more than likely saving a lot of money. Tesla needed to bring cost down. They were able to do it by making changes in their value chain, and by having the right business model in place.

Last thing we should look at about Tesla is their internal why. I mentioned their mission earlier when we were discussing how to develop your company's mission. Their mission is to accelerate the world's transition to sustainable energy. This has been a guiding light for Tesla. This is the story they tell. Everything they do is about the world getting off of nonrenewable energy from coal and oil and onto renewable energy like wind and solar. Tesla is a public company with strong alignment between its internal and external why. Because there is such close alignment, they are massively successful. They have consistently stayed true to their mission.

IKEA

IKEA is an iconic brand in the furniture market. This store is one of my favorite companies to study. They have been around for over 60 years and are still dominating the furniture market. Ikea sells high-quality, low priced furniture worldwide. There are a lot of furniture stores in the world, but no-one has been able replicate or challenge the way IKEA sells furniture. They are absolute leaders in this space.

One of the first things that should have popped out at you is the idea of "high-quality, low cost" furniture. How do they sell high quality at such low prices? In order to figure it out we only need to look in a few places. Hopefully, you know where those places are by now. Yep we are going to examine the external why; just like we did in the Tesla example. For this example, we are going to go for a day of shopping together at IKEA.

IKEA's target customers are people who are concerned with their budget but also want quality, stylish furniture. They also target people who are concerned about space as well. That's why a lot of college students love IKEA. The stores have a lot of great options that fit into compact spaces. As we discuss who Ikea's target customers are, we can clearly see what problem they solve and what end of the price spectrum they fall in. The problem is that people who are price sensitive or who are living in small spaces like apartments, usually don't have many high-quality furniture options. And of course, they are interested in the lower end of the price spectrum. As you can see, a great value proposition puts all three of its pieces together in a way that makes sense.

So how can they offer such high-quality products at such low prices? For that we need to look in their value chain. If you have ever visited an IKEA store you will immediately recognize these examples. I am going to highlight a few of the things they do in their value chain to get their quality furniture at the lower end of the price spectrum.

When you go to an Ikea store the first thing you may notice is that there are not a lot of customer service people walking around the store to help you with your selections. They have set the stores up in a way that makes the customer experience easy to navigate on your own. They do extravagant displays to show customers how the kitchen or bedroom would look all set up in their house. When you walk into one of IKEA's displays you feel like you are home. All of the options are available right there on the spot. If you actually see someone who works there, they may turn and run away. Ikea has chosen to save money by not hiring a whole lot of customer service representative to help customers on the floor. They want people to navigate the store on their own.

Next thing is that all of IKEA's product are housed in a warehouse onsite. So once you have made your selection from the beautiful displays on the floor, you write down the display number and go into the warehouse. The warehouse is connected to the display part of the store. This makes the transition seamless. Once you have your display number in hand you can walk through to the warehouse to actually get your products right then and there. You simply match the display number with the warehouse aisle number. Then you load your own stuff into your cart for check out. Again, they have limited staff available to help with this process.

Now let's talk about one of the things that sets IKEA apart from all the other furniture stores. When you walk through to the warehouse to find your stuff, you aren't getting the furniture you saw in the display. You are getting a box. IKEA makes all of their furniture to be modular. Everything from couches to bedroom sets are made so that the pieces fit in flat easy to manage boxes. This makes it so that the customer can continue creating their own shopping experience. You make your selection, then you get your merchandise all on your own. Again, this is billions of dollars Ikea is saving by not having a large staff to help with the customer experience.

Most other furniture stores don't have their furniture on site. It's kept at a warehouse that is sometimes not even in the same state as the store. Your selections get delivered to your house days or weeks after you make your purchase. In most cases the delivery people come into your house and set up the new furniture for you, and even take the old furniture away. As you can see, this experience is very different than what you get from IKEA. Traditional furniture stores have salesmen and saleswomen that meet you at the door, hand you their card, and walk you around the store asking what you may need. The cost for that kind of customer service is something that IKEA has decided not to spend. Because they don't spend this money, they can offer their furniture at a much lower cost.

Now let's move on to the checkout experience at the IKEA store. When it's time to check out you push your huge cart, with your huge box through the huge warehouse aisle, to the oversized checkout lanes. Checkout is simple, just like at a grocery store. Once you checkout you push your cart out to your car and you load your own furniture box into your car. IKEA doesn't assist with loading and they don't hold merchandise overnight for you to pick up in the morning. Their experience is set up so that you do everything on your own. From the time you walk into the store, to the time you drag the box up your front steps into your home, IKEA has made their entire value chain so that the customer creates and manages their entire experience. They literally save billions of dollars by using this value chain. All these savings put together is how they can offer such high quality, high designed furniture for such low prices.

Can you identify the areas of the value chain that IKEA focuses on? Inbound logistics, operations, and outbound logistics is where IKEA spends a lot of their resources. It's all about getting the raw furniture materials in and putting them together in a way that is easy for any customer to manage on their own. Again, the outbound logistics is set up so that the customer themselves manage that part of the value chain. They pick the furniture up, load it into their cars, and take it to their homes on their own. Another thing I'll mention to highlight how IKEA saves money is their instructions. If you have ever purchased something from IKEA, you know that when you get the box home and begin to assemble your furniture, the instructions are nothing but pictures. They make the instruction for all of their furniture boxes with very few words. This means that if you ever buy that box in America, in Germany, or in France, any customer can figure out how to put it together. IKEA saves a lot of money in having to translate instructions for the same piece of furniture into hundreds of different languages.

By taking a quick walk through IKEA, we can see exactly what their external why is. The choices they have made in their value chain to bring their value proposition to life have revolutionized the industry. IKEA decided in their value proposition who their customer was, what problem they were solving, and what end of the price spectrum they want to target. They then built an entire value chain to make it happen. All the small things they do to save money allow them to fulfill their value proposition, which is high quality, high design furniture for a very low price.

CHAPTER 10:

Business Credit

Business Credit Basics

Business credit is never talked about in the mainstream. It's like some sort of unicorn that only the special, gifted or lucky can access. But all of this is completely false. You as an early stage company or small business can have access to millions of dollars in business credit just like the big companies. The system is set up for businesses to do just that. The only thing stopping any business from establishing tier one business credit is the knowledge on how to do it. That's it. Follow my simple blueprint below and you will have virtually unlimited business credit in no time.

Business credit is completely different from your personal credit. As you probably know, the personal credit is based on your FICO score. Business credit on the other hand, is based on something called a Paydex score. Your business's Paydex score works just like the FICO score does. The higher the Paydex score, the more credit your business can get approved for. There are no tricks or special sauce; a high Paydex score opens the doors for everything. It took me years to discover the power of using business credit to fund my ideas.

Business credit is completely separate from your personal credit. This means that once you have established business credit, you can borrow money in your business's name without having to personally guarantee it. So, you can have bad personal credit and still build excellent business credit. I still think it is a good idea to fix your personal credit. I'm simply saying that you don't have to in order to build your business credit. The two do not impact each other. This was especially powerful for me because I used to fund all my business ideas with my own money and credit. There isn't anything wrong with going this route, but one mistake can set you way back with personal credit. Plus, if you use your personal credit funds, you get penalized for actually using it. I know that may sound a little confusing, but it is true. If you use up to your personal credit limit, it is viewed as a bad thing. Example, if you have a personal credit card with a $5,000 limit and you use $4,000 of it, your personal credit score will go down. It really seems a bit stupid how the system is set up. They give you the credit, then they penalize you if you use it.

Business credit is completely different. Not only are you NOT penalized for using your credit, you are encouraged to use it. They know that business credit is for businesses. Using the same example above and getting approved for $5,000 in business credit, you can use the whole thing the next day and not be penalized. You simply need to manage and maintain your monthly payments. If you use all of your available business credit but you pay your bill on time, your business credit score (Paydex score) will go up. I know you're wondering how this can be. The thing to understand about business credit is that it is based on management; while personal credit is based on utilization. This may sound small, but it is a huge deal to entrepreneurs. Basically, your personal credit is affected if you use too much of your credit limit, while your business credit is affected if you use it but don't manage it correctly (pay your bills on time).

A couple more things to know before I give you the steps for building business credit. In the world on business credit, they will take the credit away if you do not use it. Remember, when they lend money or extend credit to a business, they expect it to be used. If you get approved for business credit but never use it, they will close the account. Another thing to know is that business credit limits are much higher than personal credit limits. This is because they know that businesses are using the credit to buy inventory, equipment, marketing campaigns, etc. So, if you can get approved for $5,000 in personal credit, you could get approved for $25,000 to $50,000 on the business credit side. This happens because business credit is generally five to ten times what you would see on the personal side.

Still not convinced? Sounds too good to be true? I used to say that as well, until I actually did it for my own business. I discovered that the system is set up to help businesses, and that certain small group of people, simply know how to work the system. Once I had that realization, there was no turning back. Now I try my best to tell as many entrepreneurs as I can about how the system works. This information levels the playing field and gives every entrepreneur a better chance to succeed.

Paydex Score

As mentioned, the Paydex score for your business is the equivalent to the FICO score for you personally. This score is one of the key determining factors for business credit approval. Your personal credit FICO score can go as high as 850, and your score is generally considered good if it's over 700. On the business side, your Paydex score can go up to 100, and good scores are 80 and above. As you build your business profile, the goal is to get your business credit score up to at least an 80. This will open up most credit funding opportunities for your business.

8 Steps To Build A Business Profile

Next thing to know is that business credit approvals are based on your business profile. This means that you have to build your business profile to be considered for business credit. A business profile is your business's digital footprint that anyone can look at to decide credit worthiness. Today, everything is pretty much done electronically. A company can decide in seconds whether to give your business credit or not. They do this by looking at your credit profile. I am going to give you the steps for how to build your business credit profile. Once your business credit profile is established you can get all kinds of credit in your business's name without having to give your social security number. Once your profile is set, you will be in position to access thousand, hundreds of thousands, and even millions of dollars in business credit.

There are eight things you need to do to set up your business profile. The total cost for this process should only be a few hundred dollars. The reason is because most of these things are free. You can do them online, and they only take a few minutes. If you come across any person or website that tries to charge you to do any of these steps, please say no. Most of these steps are simple and free. Here are the steps:

1. Register your business with the Secretary of State.
2. Get an Employer Identification Number (EIN number).
3. Get a business checking account.
4. Get business address.
5. Get business phone number.

6. Get professional business email.
7. Get a business website.
8. Get a Dun and Bradstreet Number.

Ok now that you have the steps, let's go through them.

Register your business with the State

This step entails going on your states website and registering your business as an official business entity. That means you will need make your business a sole proprietorship, an LLC, an S-Corp, a C-Corp etc. Please consult with an attorney or do your own research to decide which business entity works best for your business. I cannot give you any legal or tax advice. This step will cost around $300. The exact cost depends on the state. This step is also the most expensive step.

Surprisingly, there are many entrepreneurs who start businesses without ever registering it as an official business entity with the state. This is dangerous because you need to have your business actions separate from your personal finances. Having your business officially registered can give you those kinds of protections. The last thing you want is for someone to come after your house and your kid's college fund because of something negative that has happened in your business. Again, please consult with a lawyer or do your own research to decide which entity is best for you. So not only is this the first step in building your business credit profile but it is also a necessary thing to do to protect you and your business in the future.

Get an Employee Identification Number (EIN)

First things first, getting an EIN is absolutely free. Please do not pay anyone to do this for you. All you have to do is go on the IRS website or call their 1(800) number and you can get a free EIN number. Your EIN is basically the social security number for your business. Anytime someone looks up your business, they will check your EIN number. It works almost just like your social security number does for you. You have to be officially registered with the state in order to get one of these unique EIN numbers. You have to do these first two steps in order. It's free and only takes a few minutes. Once you have your EIN, this number will stay with the business forever. It's your business's official identifying number.

Get a Business Checking Account

Step three is also easy. First, look into which bank or credit union you want to do business with. You may want to open your account with a big bank like Wells Fargo, a small bank like City National, a community bank like Farmers Community or a credit union like Navy Federal. Either way, it is totally up to you. The only information you need to open your business checking account is in the first two steps. Simply bring the information that says your business is officially registered with the state and your EIN number. These things along with your personal identification should be all you need.

Steps 4-7

The next four steps can be done in any order that you want. They are all necessary to build your business profile, but one is not dependent on the other. These are the business address, phone number, email and website. You don't absolutely have to do these steps, but I strongly recommend them to have the best chance of securing unlimited business credit. As I mentioned, just about everything is online and electronic. When companies are deciding whether to approve credit or not, they check to see if the company is at least a real business. They are not likely to give $100,000 in business credit to a home-based business being run from the living room. There's nothing wrong with home-based businesses, but they don't look professional to the company lending you the credit. That's why you should get a business address. Even if it's a virtual office. You just don't want your business address to be the same as your home address or a PO Box. Virtual offices can cost as low as $20 per month.

This same thought process is why each of the other three steps are important. When companies are considering business credit for your business, they may check your website or even call your business phone number. You want to have a business number that is different from your cellphone number. There are a bunch of inexpensive services out there that can provide you with a separate number that is different from your cell number. You can also set up a short landing page website for free or at a very low cost. The last thing in this section is the business email. There is nothing wrong with a free Gmail account, but it looks much more professional if you have an official business email. That would be your/name@xyzcompany.com. This email usually costs roughly $4 per month.

Get Your Dun and Bradstreet Number

This is the last step in setting up your business profile. I would suggest that you do the first 7 steps before you apply for the Dun and Bradstreet number, or Duns number for short. The reason is because Dun and Bradstreet is the main business credit agency. This is the actual place that will house your business profile. When you apply to get the Duns number you will need to enter all the above information to start your profile. You can change it later, but it is a headache. Also, as we discussed, it will be much easier to get approved for business credit if your profile is complete with all the other steps.

So what is Dun and Bradstreet? Dun and Bradstreet is the main reporting agency for businesses. Similar to Experian, Equifax and TransUnion on the personal credit side. When getting personal credit, the creditor checks your credit profile from one or all of these agencies. When getting business credit, your business profile on

Dun and Bradstreet is where they look. Hopefully you can see how this whole thing comes together. All the steps are there to ensure that you have a strong business credit profile on Dun and Bradstreet.

Getting the actual Duns number is also absolutely free. If you find someone trying to charge you to do this, it could possibly be a scam. You simply need to go to the website and apply. The steps are easy to follow on the website. They also have a customer support number if you have questions. Although its free, the process for getting the Duns number could take a week or two because they need to verify that your business is real and official. That's why things like being officially registered with the state are so important. Once they have verified and you have the Duns number, you are set.

Now that you have the Duns number you need to begin building your business credit profile. Just like anything you have to work your way up. Side note: the process can go a lot faster if you already have good personal credit. You can still get it done with bad personal credit, but it takes a bit longer. You can go from the beginning to getting tens of thousands of dollars in business credit in under six months if you have good personal credit. It could take you a year with bad personal credit. These timelines are general. I've seen people in many different personal situations, good and bad, do these steps in different timelines. I just want to give you some standard timelines to be thinking about.

Good Credit Folks

If you have good personal credit you can apply for credit in your business's name and use your personal credit to guarantee it. Even though you personally had to guarantee the business credit line, it does not show up on your personal credit unless you do not pay your bills. If you pay your bills on time it will only go on to your business credit profile, building it along the way. After managing that account properly for six months, you can call the lender and ask them to increase your business credit limit. You can repeat this process with a few credit lenders. Once you have multiple business credit accounts that are in good standing over six months to a year, you should be set. You would then be ready for the next step. Remember I said in the beginning that you would need to personally guarantee these accounts at first. If you follow this path you will eventually be able to apply for large credit accounts with nothing but your business EIN number. You will not have to personally guarantee the business credit accounts. If you have good personal credit to start the process you can get to this point pretty quickly. Once you have reached this level the sky is the limit.

Bad Credit Folks
(No Judgement Here, I Promise)

I have a special place in my heart for this group of people because I learned about business credit years ago with bad personal credit. Like so many entrepreneurs, some of my early business endeavors were up and down. I had some successes, but I sustained a lot of failures as well. I would use my credit to constantly get in and out of deals. One little mistake and my personal credit could easily take a 100-point hit. Sometimes I wouldn't even be doing anything wrong. I would just be utilizing the credit up to the limit, and it would negatively affect my personal credit profile. When I found out about business credit, it was groundbreaking for me. It gave me so much freedom. By the way, I didn't find this information myself. A very wealthy successful businessman told me about business credit. He said this was how the big boys do it, and it blew my mind. Of course, I have honed the process over the years, so I can now tell you about it.

If you have bad credit, it's not over. You follow all the same steps. The only thing you cannot do is personally guarantee any business credit accounts. This means you have to start at the bottom. Start with vendor accounts. Vendor accounts are accounts you can get with companies that will give you 30 days to pay your business invoices with their company. You can simply Google companies that offer net 30 vendor accounts. These companies are a great place to start because they generally extend net 30 vendor accounts to startup businesses without a personal guarantee. This means you can order things from their websites, like office supplies, and they will send you what you order right away. They will then give you 30 days to pay the bill. As you continue to do this, they will report to Dun and Bradstreet. If you do this over time with multiple companies, it will slowly build your business credit profile. Two tips for going this route. First, make sure the companies you find and apply with do report to Dun and Bradstreet (not all of them do). It does you no good if you have a net 30 vendor credit account with a company that doesn't tell Dun and Bradstreet that you are paying your bills. Second tip is that purchases under $50 do not show up on your business account. So anytime you use your account to make purchases, be sure they are at least $50.

Another way to get off the ground if you have bad personal credit are smaller "micro" type of lenders. This strategy is possible because of the times we live in. Twenty years ago, these options did not exist. Companies like PayPal and Square will lend your business thousands of dollars based solely on the money you bring in. Technology innovation has made so many of these kinds of options available for entrepreneurs. They also have business credit cards that are geared toward start-up businesses and even entrepreneurs who have bad credit. Definitely look to find some vendor accounts for your business, but you may want to also look up these smaller online business lenders that cater specifically to start-up and small businesses. If you consistently follow this strategy over time, you will eventually be able to apply for business credit without having to personally guarantee it. Again, once you get there the sky is the limit!

CHAPTER 11:

I Just Want to Help

(Entrepreneur Bonus Tips)

This chapter is dedicated to a few bonus tips that all entrepreneurs need to know. It doesn't matter where you are in your business, these tips can help you. I was years into my business before I began discovering some of these tips. The large successful companies know these things. They also teach this stuff at Harvard and Stanford business schools. The problem with this is that most entrepreneurs will never get an MBA from Harvard. However, they should be able to have access to this groundbreaking information. I want all entrepreneurs to be able to take advantage of the system and leverage it for their good.

The Elevator Pitch

As an investor Vision to Value gives me a tremendous amount of confidence when assessing potential opportunities. I love when entrepreneurs can clearly articulate their business. Entrepreneurs must be able to clearly and concisely talk about their business and ideas. I've seen business coaches teach the "elevator pitch" to entrepreneurs. There is nothing wrong with the elevator pitch, but I want to give you a bit more practical perspective. Essentially, the elevator pitch is a quick and often memorized statement that you can rattle off if you ever need to. I've never been a huge fan of the elevator pitch because it always seems forced and a bit contrived. I guess you do need to be prepared for when you are trapped in an elevator with Oprah for a minute while she rides up to her penthouse in the hotel you are also staying in. The problem is that, although it could happen, this is a very unlikely.

Instead, I use Vision to Value to teach my students how to simply and intelligently discuss their business with anyone. I think it's much better to be conversational about your business. Be concise, but be able to talk someone through what you do. The way to do this is by utilizing the principles of the Vision to Value framework. Instead of an elevator pitch all you need is the main pieces of your external and internal why. If you get into an "elevator pitch" situation, clearly tell your customers why and then tell your why. That's your value proposition and your vision. For anyone who wants to know about your business, this is always where you start. Remember all business starts here anyway. They need to know why your customers choose your business, and why you are committed to the business. That's it. So instead of trying to memorize an elevator pitch, just be able to clearly and concisely state your external and internal why.

If you still decide to craft a formal elevator pitch, that's totally alright. You never know when you might get caught in the elevator with Oprah. For all the other times, simply knowing the why of your business gives you great context for any business conversation.

Failing Forward

I would be doing you a disservice in writing a book to entrepreneurs without discussing failure. This topic is important no matter where you are in your journey. The first and most important thing you must do as an entrepreneur, is change your relationship with failure. Over 70% of all new businesses fail within the first 3 years. That means that the odds are stacked against you from the beginning. Any successful entrepreneur will tell you that failure is a big part of success. Every failure is an opportunity to learn about your business and your industry in the real world.

Real world experience is one of the most valuable assets of an entrepreneur. I'm sure you've heard successful people talk about how they had failed their way to success. Understanding the role failure will play in your ultimate success as an entrepreneur will put you miles ahead of everyone else. Just the sheer acceptance that failure is a part of the journey will give you a competitive advantage. This will give you the mental fortitude you need to look at a failure and immediately see learning and growth for your next opportunity. To be clear, failure sucks. Nobody wants to fail at business or anything. The problem is that everyone will fail at something. When it comes to business, those statistics are overwhelming.

So what can you do as an entrepreneur to help with failure? The first thing you can do is prepare. You must be prepared when you go into any business. The Vision to Value framework is a great tool you can take into any business opportunity, to increase the likelihood of success. The second thing is something that I mentioned earlier, which is change your relationship with failure. From today on, make a conscious effort to view failure as a learning opportunity. Find something about the negative experience to gain from. This paradigm shift of thinking is guaranteed to push you into success, if you stay positive and continue to move forward.

About the Author

Tremain Davis is an entrepreneur with 20 years of business experience. He has founded 3 companies and invested in a handful of others. He now teaches entrepreneurship on the university level and has been a strategy consultant for hundreds of companies.

Tremain's entrepreneurial career started in 2001 when he left his college basketball scholarship on the table, in his second year, to found his first tech company. He built a sports recruitment platform which was one of the first in its space. Tremain and his team were working on "streaming video" as a service three years before YouTube was created. Tremain's second company was an investment consulting company in Atlanta, Georgia. During this time, Tremain's firm did over $30 million in business in the areas of real estate and technology.

In 2011, Tremain founded Davis and Davis Investments and Management, which he still operates today. Davis and Davis is a boutique strategy consulting firm focused on innovative technologies and real estate utilization strategies. Davis and Davis is based in the Washington, D.C. metropolitan area, where Tremain also resides, and serves hundreds of clients. Tremain has also pioneered a new success framework based on his years of business strategy expertise. He has taught his "Vision to Value Entrepreneurial Framework" at institutions like Howard University, Virginia Tech University, Bowie State University, United Negro College Fund, and Prince Georges Community College.

Tremain realizes that small businesses are the absolute backbone of our economy, and that entrepreneurs need better tools to be successful. He wrote this book to give a step-by-step blueprint that any entrepreneur, anywhere, can follow for business success. He doesn't want to just tell his story of success. He wants to empower entrepreneurs to take their ideas to the next level.

To learn more about Tremain Davis, please visit: www.tremaindavis.net.

www.ingramcontent.com/pod-product-compliance
Lightning Source LLC
Chambersburg PA
CBHW031121210326
41519CB00047B/4182